Practical Induction

Elijah Millgram

Practical Induction

Harvard University Press
Cambridge, Massachusetts
London, England
1997

Library of Congress Cataloging-in-Publication Data
Millgram, Elijah.
  Practical induction / Elijah Millgram.
    p.   cm.
  Includes bibliographical references (p.   ) and index.
  ISBN 0-674-69597-6 (alk. paper)
  1. Reasoning.   2. Induction (Logic)   I. Title.
BC177.M52   1997
161—dc20
96-41362

Acknowledgments

In writing this book, I have benefited from the generous assistance of many people. Hilary Bok, Michael Bratman, Sam Fleischacker, Henry Richardson, Candace Vogler, and reviewers for Harvard University Press read through an earlier draft of the entire manuscript and provided very helpful comments. Among those who read and gave me comments on one or another version of one or more chapters were: Alyssa Bernstein, John Broome, Sarah Buss, Arthur Collins, Alice Crary, Julia Driver, Christoph Fehige, Konstanze Feigel, Harry Frankfurt, Tamar Gendler, Jean Hampton, Gil Harman, Wilfried Hinsch, Jenann Ismael, Mark Johnston, Rachana Kamtekar, Harold Langsam, Ariela Lazar, Mitzi Lee, David Lewis, Beatrice Longuenesse, Gloria Park, Christian Piller, Emily Rosenzweig, Jennifer Saul, Geoff Sayre-McCord, Sydney Shoemaker, Michael Slote, Bill Talbott, Manuel Utset, Gregory Vlastos, and Bernard Williams. (My apologies if I've missed anyone.) Gabriel Richardson proofread the manuscript. Without their unstinting and thoughtful responses, this would have been a very different book.

This book is the descendant of a doctoral dissertation supervised by Hilary Putnam, Robert Nozick, and Tim Scanlon, to whom I'm grateful for guidance, patience, and very constructive criticism. An earlier version of Chapter 2 appears in *Preferences*, edited by Christoph Fehige and Ulla Wessels; my thanks to Walter de Gruyter & Co. for permission to reprint, and to audiences at CUNY, Yale, the University of Waterloo,

Ben-Gurion University, and the conference that originated the *Preferences* volume for stimulating discussion. An earlier version of Chapter 6, titled "Pleasure in Practical Reasoning", appeared in *The Monist* (Copyright © 1993, *The Monist*, La Salle, Illinois 61301.) Reprinted by permission.

I would like to dedicate this book to the memory of Sarah Crome and Gregory Vlastos, who, in quite different ways, were counterexamples to the views argued here.

Contents

I

Introduction

Practical reasoning is reasoning whose point is to control decision or action; it is contrasted with theoretical reasoning, which aims at figuring out how things stand, rather than at doing something about them. Deciding to eat the spinach because it's rich in iron and you mean to have more iron in your diet would be an example of some not-very-momentous practical reasoning. In this book I am going to argue that practical reasoning, when it is done properly, is driven by experience: that part of practical reasoning is learning, from experience, what matters and what is important.

This claim might seem obvious—so obvious, in fact, as to be hardly worth arguing for at all. So I'm going to begin by explaining how it is that this obvious fact has come to seem not simply false but counterintuitive and wrongheaded to many philosophers, and why it's important to get straight about it. With these explanations in place, I'll go on to sketch a quick road map of the argument.

Why is practical reasoning worth investigating in the first place? There are both direct and indirect benefits to be had from understanding how practical reasoning works. Just as studying logic can improve your arguments and the beliefs they give rise to, so studying practical reasoning might improve your deliberations, your decisions, and your actions. Less directly, because theories of practical reasoning have consequences for ethics, for philosophy of mind, and for political philosophy, an interest in these subjects gives rise to a derivative interest in understanding the workings of practical reasoning. We can get some idea of how a theory of practical reasoning can have consequences in these areas by considering what is more or less the received view of the subject: instrumentalism.

Instrumentalism is the view that all practical reasoning is means-end reasoning. It says that there are various things you want, and the point of practical reasoning is to figure out how to get them. Instrumentalism is an exclusionist view: if it is right, then while you can think about how to get what you want, you can't think about what to want in the first place. Put this way, instrumentalism might not sound like a very convincing theory: after all, most of us seem to do a certain amount of thinking about what to want (in philosophical jargon, 'deliberation of ends'), and actually doing it should be good evidence that we *can*. I'll say a little more about what makes instrumentalism an attractive theory shortly; right now, I want to indicate what is likely to happen if you believe it.

Because moral reasoning is practical reasoning, a moral philosopher's view of practical reasoning is likely to shape the development of his moral theory. Instrumentalists think that practical reasoning proceeds from desires that are not themselves revisable by reasoning. These are desires that you just happen to have, and we can say that they are *arbitrary*. Consequently, instrumentalists working in ethics are likely to encounter the following problem. On the one hand, morality ought to be rationally motivating; but, on the other hand, all rational motivation proceeds from arbitrary desires. How can an instrumentalist moral theorist show that it is rational to be moral, given that people might have amoral, immoral or perverse desires? One approach might be to argue that people in fact *do* have moral desires. (This is a way Hume's discussion of sympathy has been taken.)[1] Another might be to argue that rational self-interest can provide a bridge from the not particularly moral desires you happen to have to moral action. (Hobbes can be read in this way, and, not that long ago, this was how Aristotle's *Nicomachean Ethics* was taught.)[2] Or again, desires could be run through something like a

---

1. Although Hume is widely taken to have been an instrumentalist, I have argued elsewhere that he was not (1995b). The problem to which sympathy is meant to be a solution is, however, shared by instrumentalism and the view Hume actually had.

2. I'll refer to the *Ethics* by *NE* and line number.

filter: only those desires passing, say, a universalization test will count as bases for rational (or moral) action. (Kant is sometimes interpreted as having a theory of this kind.) Approaches to the problem differ, but whatever the approach, if a moral theorist is trying to address the instrumentalist problem of arbitrary desires, this is bound to affect the shape of the resulting moral theory. If the problem of arbitrary desires arises in the context of instrumentalism, and if instrumentalism turns out to be a mistake, then the ways in which the problem shapes moral theories will have to be counted as unhappy distortions. If you care about having the right moral theory, you should also care about having the right theory of practical reasoning.

Theories of practical reasoning also tend to shape views in philosophy of mind and moral psychology, by determining, for example, what features of which mental states are seen as central for explaining and reconstructing thought. Philosophers do not find out what people's thoughts look like by examining the contents of their skulls. Rather, they interpret subjects' speech and behavior; and this means that what they see is in significant part an artifact of the theory of rationality they bring to bear in the process of interpretation. Once again, consider instrumentalism. Instrumental reasoning that leads to, and so explains, action invokes only desires, and beliefs about ways to attain those desires. ('If you desire a hat, and you believe that if you give the man behind the counter the money he will give you a hat, then you have a reason to give him the money.') It is hard not to suspect that the prominence that beliefs and desires have in contemporary philosophical pictures of the mind (so-called 'belief-desire psychology') is due to a background view of practical reasoning that highlights beliefs and desires at the expense of emotions, visual imagery, fantasies, dreams, and other familiar residents of the human soul. If belief-desire psychology is mistaken, the best way to correct it is to correct the theory of practical reasoning that underwrites it; once again, if you care about having a satisfactory picture of the mind, you should care about having a satisfactory theory of practical reasoning.

Finally, a widely accepted view of practical reasoning can influence both political philosophy and practical politics by determining what forms of political argument are regarded as legitimate. For example, by insisting that one can reason about how to attain the ends one already has, but not about what one's ends should be in the first place, instrumentalism legitimizes the powerful in directing their intellectual energies into thinking about how to advance their interests, and away from considering whether those interests should be broadened or curtailed. Not only does instrumentalism fail to provide a way to criticize the ends of those in power, it denies the downtrodden one of the strongest claims they can make against an existing social order: that it works to prevent the development of the aims, goals, and aspirations that, in the normal course of rational deliberation, they would make their own. So there are political reasons to care about having the right theory of practical reasoning as well.

I've been gesturing at the range of effects that an instrumentalist theory of practical reasoning is likely to have as a way of making the general point that having the right theory of practical reasoning matters. But instrumentalism is more than just *a* theory of practical reasoning: it is a very widely accepted theory of practical reasoning. This isn't the place for the kind of survey that would be needed to back up this claim properly; but one can get a sense of how deeply entrenched it is by glancing at Robert Audi's *Practical Reasoning,* a recent volume whose dust jacket announces that it is part of a series "intended to be intelligible to undergraduates in philosophy." Consistent with the aims of the series, it surveys the history and current state of the field, in the course of which Audi tries to present the received view rather than advance especially controversial claims of his own. And, as he puts it, his "point of departure is the view that practical reasoning is very broadly a kind of means-end reasoning."[3] Audi does not find it necessary to argue for instrumentalism, or even to mention alternatives. This is a very good indication of the extent to which contemporary philosophers feel that they can simply take instrumentalism for granted.

Instrumentalism can seem to be an attractive, even inevitable, theory. It has the feel of hard-headed, tough-minded realism: How could anything be a reason for action if it could not motivate you to actually *do* something? And what could motivate you to do something except

---

3. Audi, 1989, p. 146; see also pp. 89, 95f, 98f, 131. Of course, the author should not be held responsible for the jacket copy.

one of your desires? It seems refreshingly honest: People who try to convince you to do things you don't want to do are, too often, just trying to bully you into doing something you don't really have any reason to do at all. Instrumentalism seems to give you a very convenient way to distinguish this kind of browbeating from real reasons to act: real reasons bottom out in what you want anyway.[4] And instrumentalism seems to be metaphysically respectable, where the arbiter of respectability in the relevant circles is a broadly-shared image of science. Desires are psychological states, and there is no problem in making room for psychological states among the particles, organisms, causal regularities, and other items that we encounter in science textbooks; or so it is supposed, the contrary opinion of Descartes notwithstanding.[5] And there is in principle no problem in explaining how we come to know what desires are had by whom. The same cannot be said, however, about values, the Good, the rightness of some actions as opposed to others, and other such creatures from the far side of the fact-value distinction. These, it is claimed, are metaphysically mysterious or 'queer', and, in the right mood, can come to seem like the characters in a philosophical fairy tale, one that instrumentalism is too no-nonsense to have any truck with.[6]

But instrumentalism is incompatible with the claim this book is going to advance: if instrumentalism is true, experience cannot teach you what matters. On the instrumentalist view, you do not want things because they matter; rather, they matter because you want them. (Instrumentalism accounts for our sense that we try to figure out what we want, and that part of this process is figuring out what really matters, by suggesting that we are confusing figuring out what we ultimately want with figuring out what we want and what matters *derivatively*, that is, as a

---

4. Bernard Williams develops these lines of argument in his influential paper, "Internal and External Reasons", 1981a. For discussion, see Millgram, 1996.

5. There are contemporary contrary opinions too. See, for example, Stich, 1983, Collins, 1987.

6. Mackie, 1983, ch. 1. This is not to say that instrumentalists have to end up denying that there are values, right actions, and so on. The usual strategy is to attempt to reconstruct these notions in terms of desires; e.g., by defining right action as that action which best satisfies desires, or values in terms of what one desires (or under optimal circumstances would desire) to desire.

way of attaining what we ultimately want.) Since I will be arguing for an incompatible view, I will need to take a stand against instrumentalism sooner or later, and, for tactical reasons, I propose to do it sooner.[7] So in Chapter 2 I will argue that instrumentalism must be wrong anyway, for reasons that have nothing to do with the possibility of learning what matters from experience. Having shown that instrumentalism is mistaken, we will be in a position to consider an alternative to it; this alternative I will call *practical induction.*

Practical induction is the practical analog of inductive reasoning. Inductive reasoning is familiar from such inferences as: 'All the ravens I have ever seen have been black, so, probably, all ravens are black.' Like the more familiar forms of inductive reasoning, practical induction moves from instances to generalizations, and, also like them, it bottoms out in experience. In Chapter 3, I will lay out the contribution that practical induction makes to unity of agency, and argue that if its contribution is indispensable, then practical induction is a legitimate form of inference. In Chapter 4, I will show that its contribution *is* indispensable: there are no workable alternatives to practical induction. And in Chapter 5, I will explain why the argument of Chapters 3 and 4 works. The idea behind the argument is a simple one: we must be able to learn new interests from experience because we encounter new and unfamiliar situations. Genuine novelty is an inescapable feature of our world. In novel circumstances, the desires, aims, and interests we already have are too often suddenly obsolete. In order to have the guides to action that we need, we have to allow new circumstances to teach us what to care about. If we do not, we will cease to project unified agency into the world, and that is enough to show practical induction to be a legitimate method of inference.

Accepting practical induction as a legitimate form of inference raises the question of where such inferences get their premises. For the more traditional sort of inductions, you can find premises in two ways: you can look and see for yourself (experience or observation), and you can rely on what others tell you (testimony). So in the following two chapters, I will consider whether observation and testimony have practical

---

7. I will not be surveying the standard menu of instrumentalist moves here. I discuss the most common of these in Millgram, 1996.

or decision-oriented forms. I will argue that they do, and that they are closely connected with pleasure and friendship, respectively. This stretch of the argument comes with fringe benefits. In the course of explaining practical observation, an account of what pleasure is will emerge that shows what is wrong with hedonism. And a discussion of the way friendship arises from trust in others' testimony will provide a new way of taking Aristotle's pronouncement that the friend is another self.

Before diving into the argument, I need to flag a bit of terminology, and to mention some of the things I'm *not* going to do. Terminology first: I'm going to use the word 'practical' to mean that what is being described has to do with practical reasoning. And, following one fairly standard usage, I'm going to use the contrasting term 'theoretical' to indicate that what is being described has to do with theoretical reasoning, that is, reasoning whose point is to arrive at an opinion as to the facts, rather than a decision about what to do. This (occasionally awkward) usage dictates that 'theoretical' should not be understood to imply contrasts that invoke the notion of a theory, and that 'practical' should not be understood to entail 'applied', 'down-to-earth', or 'not impractical'.

On to the disclaimers. First, while instrumentalism is an exclusionist doctrine, the view I will be advancing is not. In arguing for the legitimacy of practical induction, I don't mean to suggest that it is the only form that practical reasoning can take. Means-end reasoning is of course a kind of practical reasoning, even if it is not the only kind. There are other alternatives to instrumentalism already in the field, most notably Kantian views, which emphasize the universalizability of intentions, and specificationist theories (sometimes attributed to Aristotle), which consider how vaguely conceived ends can be rendered more concrete and precise. (I am leaving these out of the discussion not because I do not think they are worth discussing, but because others have done so; anyone who has not yet been convinced of the merits of these views by the defenders they already have is not going to be convinced by me.)[8] And finally, I believe there are other forms of practical reasoning that have

---

8. For Kant's views, see Kant, 1785/1981, Nell, 1974, Korsgaard, 1990. Representatives of specificationism include Kolnai, 1978, Wiggins, 1980, Broadie, 1987, and Richardson, 1994. Although I will not argue for or against specificationism, I will briefly consider a consequence of my arguments for the view in section 6.7.

not been on the traditional menu, such as the practical analog of resolving contradictions in one's system of beliefs; I will not discuss those here either.[9]

Second, I'm not going to talk about the loosely demarcated body of mathematics that goes under the name of decision theory. This might seem surprising, since there is a part of it—expected utility theory— that some philosophers treat as though it were a technical reformulation of the instrumentalist theory of practical reasoning.[10] But if expected utility theory really is instrumentalism made rigorous, then it is, for my purposes, sufficiently addressed by the argument of Chapter 2, while if it is not, I am, once again, comfortable leaving the topic to others.

Third, many discussions of practical reasoning focus on questions such as: What is the nature of practical reasoning? What mental states (desires, intentions, ought-judgments, and so on) are involved in it? What are the elements of a practical inference? Not only will I not try to answer these questions, I will try very hard to avoid presupposing any very definite answers to them. Partly I will do this so that I can make headway on answering the questions about patterns of practical inference that are at the top of my agenda. And partly I will do this because I think that attempts to answer these questions are premature. The more general questions—like, what is practical reasoning, and how exactly does it differ from theoretical reasoning?—are best postponed until we know a little more about what the territory of practical reasoning actually looks like. Such questions should be answered bottom up, rather than top down; top-down philosophy tends to turn preconceptions into constraints on what would count as an acceptable theory, and so makes it hard to see anything one doesn't already think is there. And we have reason to put the more particular questions on the back burner as well. Recall my earlier suggestion that accounts of the mental are read off of theories of inference. If this suggestion is correct, questions about the mental states involved in practical inference, and about the logical status of the contents of those states, should be deferred until we understand what the patterns of practical inference in which they figure are.

---

9. See Thagard and Millgram, 1995; Millgram and Thagard, 1996.

10. For the canonical exposition of expected utility theory, see Luce and Raiffa, 1957.

We will not be in a position to say whether we do our practical reasoning with desires, or intentions, or evaluative beliefs (to name just three often-discussed options), or whether what they express are imperatives, or descriptions of values, or something else, until we are much farther down the road.

Finally, I will, for very similar reasons, stay as far away as possible from questions having to do with the metaphysics of value: what values are, whether they are distinct from facts, whether they depend on desires, whether they are objective, and so on. As with mental states, our understanding of values is largely derived from our understanding of practical reasoning, which means that substantive views about value are likely to beg questions if they're used in an argument about what forms practical reasoning can take. It also means, however, that if we can successfully avoid invoking them until the argument is over, we may be in a better position to answer some of the old questions about value.

2

Deciding to Desire

It is a fact, and, I will argue, not merely an empirical or accidental or contingent fact, that, in at least a very broad range of cases, one cannot desire at will—that is, that one cannot simply come to have desires in the way one might raise one's arm. That it *is* a fact was noticed by Hutcheson, who pointed out that "neither benevolence nor any other affection or desire can be directly raised by volition"; if they could, he reasoned, there would be a market for affections and desires.[1] In this chapter I'm going to use this fact to show that instrumentalism, the view that the only form that practical reasoning can take is means-end reasoning, must be mistaken.

The argument will be directed toward the following aspect of instrumentalism. Means-end reasoning, on the instrumentalist view, bottoms out in whatever desires one happens to have; any way of being more selective about the desires one can legitimately use as inferential starting points would amount to admitting a form of practical reasoning that was not means-end reasoning. Only desires count, and so desires have to count simply in virtue of being desires.

But desires cannot count, simply in virtue of being desires, if we are to think with them. And it is the requirement that the mental states

---

1. In Raphael, 1969, vol. 1, p. 274. It may be thought naive to assume that there is no market of this kind. But notice that what passes for it involves deception, both of oneself and of others, that would be unnecessary were desiring at will a straightforward matter of voluntary action.

of which a mind is composed be such as to allow them to add up to a mind—equivalently, be the kinds of things with which one can think—that explains the incapacity that is our point of entry into the argument.

§ 2.1

We are all familiar with the fact that there are fairly severe restrictions on desiring at will. The marriage foundering on a lack of sensual desire will not be salvaged by determining to *have* such a desire, and there is nothing to be gained by the other party's insisting that one *try*. Presented with a hideous ceramic gewgaw, I cannot, with the best will in the world, please my misguided relative by actually *wanting* the thing. Similarly, we cannot, by the sheer exercise of will, bring about the cessation of desire: it is cold comfort to the disappointed applicant to point out that one need merely abandon one's desires in order to be content. This independence of desire from volition requires a more precise formulation, which must wait on the subsequent argument. But it is clear that in quite a wide range of cases one cannot decide to desire and come to have the desire as an unmediated consequence of the decision.

After we have made some headway in the argument, we will be in a much better position to make decisions about how to understand the notoriously plastic words 'want' and 'desire'; in the meantime, something needs to be said about what they indicate.[2] I will use them interchangably, to pick out attitudes constituted by the (largely practical) inferential commitments of their possessor. As Anscombe has remarked, the primitive sign of wanting is trying to get; a somewhat less primitive sign is inferring, for example, that in order to get, one had better first get something else.[3] To desire is not necessarily to make such inferences, nor

---

2. I'm going to ignore uses such as the commendatory 'really wants', which indicates not a state that one is in, but, for example, a state one would be in were one correctly to deliberate; the desires relevant in a discussion of instrumentalism are those available to the agent at the outset of his deliberations.

3. Anscombe, 1985, sec. 36. Bear in mind that the inferences I have in mind are not merely hypothetical: wanting X is not a matter of idly realizing that in order to get X, I would have to get Y, but of being committed to draw the conclusion that I had better get Y.

indeed to act; but it is to be committed to making such inferences in the appropriate circumstances.[4]

The terminological choice is appropriate if only because our eventual target is instrumentalism, which is, among other things, a view about the inferential role desires play; but this use of 'desire' is not out of line with our ordinary ways of speaking. A putative desire that fails to exert leverage on one's practical reasoning—that does not, even in the absence of competing considerations, even in a situation most immediately presenting the opportunity for satisfaction, require some practical inference of its possessor—must matter in a way that is quite different from a desire that does have inferential consequences. So it is not surprising that common usage traces the distinction. We generally say of someone who claims to have a desire, but denies the legitimacy of such inferential demands (even when there are no competing considerations, and the circumstances are otherwise favorable), that he does not seem actually to have the desire after all. If we use the term 'orectic state' to denote psychological states that seem to involve an attraction to their objects, we can say that there are orectic states other than desire, and that perhaps he has misclassified his. It may be a wish or a fantasy.[5] It may be a whim, a passing fancy. Or it may be an urge, understood as something like an alienated bit of sensation, the orectic analog of what one recognizes as an hallucination: an appearance resembling others that are inferentially

---

4. A good deal falls under the heading of appropriateness, for example, the presence of other competing and overriding desires; I won't now try to give an account of what is involved here. This construal of desires should not be confused with a behaviorist or functionalist analysis. To be committed to an inference or action is not *simply* to be disposed to draw the inference or produce the specified behavior. The akratic, or weak-willed individual, acknowledges his commitments, but fails to live up to them; he not only fails to make the practical inferences to which he is committed, but makes inferences whose legitimacy he denies. Of course, inferential and behavioral dispositions are important evidence, and perhaps important constituents, of inferential commitments; but I do not propose to attempt to spell out the relation between them here.

5. On wishes, see Anscombe, 1985, sec. 36; Lear, 1990, pp. 75–84. Fantasies seem to play a part in our emotional economy that has little to do with practical inference; often they are themselves satisfying, and they need not direct one to their objects. One may immerse oneself in fantasies of situations that one is aware would be found entirely unappealing were they to be presented as actual options. (For this point, I'm indebted to Elizabeth Calihan.)

related to one's beliefs, but which is not itself so related. (This taxonomy is of course not meant to be exhaustive.) In any case, it is not a desire; desires have inferential consequences.

Our examples are enough to remind us that in many cases (I will later suggest, the principled majority of cases) one cannot desire at will. But it might still seem that this is just an accident, or at any rate, a merely contingent and not particularly deep fact—one for which, say, an evolutionary explanation might be given. (Think of the things people might do to themselves if they could *really* control their desires: victims of ascetic ideologies would quite routinely starve themselves to death, or commit suicide for the greater glory of God; the indolent would replace their demanding desires for well-raised progeny with more easily satisfied wants; and the attitudes that guide life would be even more the prey of destructive fashion than they are now.) If this were so, there would perhaps be little of philosophical, as opposed to anthropological, interest to be learned by considering it.

If, however, the restrictions on desiring at will *were* contingent, and something like the evolutionary explanation were correct, it would be possible in principle, with sufficiently exotic technology, to circumvent them. (Similarly, there are good evolutionary reasons why we cannot prevent conception at will, but this lack can be technologically remedied.) We may dramatize the possibility by imagining a pharmaceutical industry that manufactures a range of pills producing desires that p, for arbitrary values of p. We can call coming to have a desire by taking such a pill, 'desiring at pill'.[6] Showing that 'desiring at pill' is not possible when desiring at will is not would show that the severe restrictions on desiring at will that we are considering are not merely contingent.

So, in order to show that desiring at will, or more generally, deciding to desire, is not merely contingently beyond our powers in these cases, I will argue that 'desiring at pill' is itself subject to similar restrictions. More precisely, I will argue that indirect techniques of intentionally acquiring desires are ineffective in the same way that indirect methods of acquiring beliefs are—that is, that they are ineffective *unless* certain conditions are imposed upon the process. Examining these conditions will

6. This turn of phrase is due to Bill Haines.

show the restrictions on both desiring at will and 'desiring at pill' to be not merely contingent, and will put us in a position to say just what the restrictions in question really are.

While a suitable specification of the conditions in question must await an explanatory account of the phenomenon, let me try to give a rough indication of the kind of thing I have in mind. Bernard Williams has discussed a fact that is closely related to the one we are considering, namely, that it is impossible to believe at will; and he has argued that indirect means of believing at will (paying a hypnotist to make one believe might be an instance of such an indirect means) can be effective only if, for example, one forgets that one did such a thing.[7] Similarly, indirect means of desiring at will (for instance, paying a hypnotist to induce the desire, or taking a desire-inducing pill) can be effective only if, for example, one forgets that one acquired the desire in this way, or one comes to think that one has reasons, broadly understood, that support the desire in the way that an ordinarily acquired desire might be supported, or one suffers a failure of rationality.[8] This is not an exhaustive list of restrictions, and I will discuss others below.

If one starts down the path of filling out the list of conditions that must be satisfied for believing at will to be possible, the outline of something like the following condition on acquiring belief starts to present itself: one cannot take it that one has acquired and is maintaining a belief in a way that one takes to provide no reason to hold it true. I'm going to argue that there are analogous restrictions on desiring at will, and this is bound to suggest that there is some very similar condition to be teased out of the parallel constraints on deciding to desire.

Now one might doubt that there could be such constraints. After all, it is widely thought that one *just has* desires—one can give causal ac-

---

7. Williams, 1973a. His claim has generated a literature that qualifies it in ways that follow the rough outline of the conditions I will describe below; see, e.g., Winters, 1979, Cook, 1987.

8. This last clause may appear to pose the danger of trivializing the claim, but I think the sequel will show that it does not. It is addressed primarily to cases of this kind: I will suggest that the realization that one has acquired a desire by decision normally undermines that desire. But the desire need not be undermined when that realization is lacking, and the explanation for this need not lie in a failure of memory. Sometimes one fails, for whatever reason, to put two and two together.

counts of how one came to have them, but not reasons that support them in the way that, say, evidence supports belief. (Instrumental reasons may be thought to be an exception to the arationality or blindness of desire. But justifying a desire by showing its object to be a means of satisfying some further desire brings one around, sooner or later, to a desire one just *has*.) Desires, on this view, are distinguished from beliefs by their 'direction of fit': while beliefs are responsible to the world, and are mistaken if they do not conform to the way the world is, desires are that to which one tries to make the world conform. They are responsible to nothing and cannot be mistaken; there is nothing in the ambit of desire to play the role that truth plays in the sphere of belief. If the claimed constraints on desiring at will are going to amount to a requirement that one take oneself to have reasons for one's desires, then there can be no such constraints.

I intend to run this argument in the other direction. Demonstrating restrictions on the indirect acquisition of desires would strongly support the claim that a desire is not something that one just has. And from this it will follow that positions—like instrumentalism—which are committed to that claim cannot be correct.

§ 2.2

To establish that there are restrictions on desiring at will it was sufficient to examine a few examples. Similarly, reviewing examples will suffice to establish that there are restrictions on the indirect acquisition of desires, and that one cannot just acquire any desire 'at pill'.

> I wish to become an automobile salesman in a future in which purportedly desire-producing pills are available. In order to get the job, and to perform well in it, I have to be genuinely enthusiastic about expensive options that I now think are at best a waste of money: the electric moonroof, the talking seatbelt, the EuroStripe trim package, the retractable headlights, the rotating hood ornament. I have read in the salesman's bible that enthusiasm of this order means, among other things, that I have to desire these options myself, and desire them strongly enough to find them not just worth the money, but a bargain at this, or almost any,

price. I want the job, and because car salesmen work on commission, I want to do well on the job. So I take a pill that is supposed to induce in me the requisite desires.

Suddenly, recession strikes: car sales go down, and I am laid off. And shortly thereafter, in a special promotion, my previous employers offer me a deal on a Honda Ferrett. Though the car itself is going for full price, I will be given a steep discount on the options. I *seem* (we are supposing for now that the pill is this effective) enthusiastically to desire the electric moonroof and so on. If I really want these things, if they matter that much to me, I can afford them. Will I—should I—plunk down the money for the Ferrett?

As I deliberate, surely I am bound to recall that I have these 'desires' only because I took a pill, and that I took the pill for entirely job-related reasons. Indeed, I had originally thought these things not worth desiring. This is still a substantial amount of money, not to be thrown away on a whim. I would be *crazy* to act on these 'desires' now. Perhaps these thoughts will suffice fully to undo the effects of the pill. Or perhaps there will be residual effects that I shall resolutely ignore. In any case, I will politely decline to make the purchase.

Two features of this example deserve attention. First, if we bear in mind the way in which the term 'desire' is here being used, we see that the pill does not work as advertised: it does not induce desire, for desires involve inferential commitments, and these turn out to be lacking. And second, there is always the possibility that the second thoughts just out-lined will not occur to me, or will seem somehow unimportant. (Perhaps this is a side-effect of the pill.) But if they do not, my family and friends will think, and quite properly too, that I do not have my head screwed on right; such an oversight, or such failure to appreciate the force of sec-ond thoughts like these, would be a *cognitive* failure.

Here is another example. As Aristotle noted, one desires the good for one's friend for the friend's own sake; such desires, not themselves dependent on ulterior motives, are constituents of friendship. This is not to say that one cannot have reasons for these desires; only that enough of them must not be the instrumental reasons that would amount to ulterior motives. But one may have extrinsic reasons for having friends, too; as Aristotle also noted, friends are the greatest external good.

> Pursuant to my desire not to dine alone, I decide to acquire a friend. In order to accelerate the normally rather gradual process of developing a friendship, I and my similarly-motivated partner (someone I have found through the classified personals) agree to take pills that will induce (among other things) desires for each other's welfare. Now we are, it seems, friends.
>
> Or are we? The next day my 'friend' is taken severely ill; I discover that he will spend the rest of his life unable to leave his nursing home. My 'friend' would very much like to be visited, so my apparent desire for his welfare expresses itself in an inclination to spend my evenings by his bedside. But I am bound to recall that I acquired this apparent desire only as a means to spending pleasant evenings dining out. Nursing homes are unpleasant, and the food is bad; why on earth am I acting on this desire? I will leave my partner to his fate. I have turned out to be, not a friend, but a fair-weather friend.

The example shows once again that 'desiring at pill' doesn't work; the 'desire' fades as its inferential consequences are suppressed.[9] Did I really have the desire? Not if a desire is, first and foremost, something that plays a certain kind of role in practical inference. A desire is something that makes certain inferential demands; for example, it is something that, ceteris paribus, I take it that I should act on, something whose object I try to obtain. But I don't take these putative desires to underwrite such demands, and therefore they cannot really be my desires. Once again, I fail to have these desires because I realize that drawing inferences from them would be unreasonable; it is my awareness of the craziness of acting

---

9. It also shows that friendship is more interesting, and harder to provide a philosophical account of, than might have been supposed. There must be more to friendship than this admittedly very important desire, and what more there is must explain how this desire can be stable in a way that pill-induced desires are not. We will return to this subject in Chapter 7.

on the desire that prevents it from sticking. Evidently, deciding to desire doesn't work *because* it would be irrational.[10]

One might object that these examples do not make the point I want. My claim that what the pill has induced is not really a desire after all ignores the ceteris paribus aspect of the inferential commitments involved in desire. I act on, and draw inferences from, my desires, only when other things are equal; and here they are not. If I don't buy the Ferrett, it's because I have better things to do with the money; and if money were no object, or were less of an object, I would go ahead and make the purchase.

This objection, however, won't do. Recall the ceramic gewgaw bestowed upon me by my relative. I wish to be a gracious recipient of gifts, so I swallow my distaste and accept it; but then, do I not really want it after all? Perhaps there is a sense in which I do, but common sense tells us that we can distinguish this desire from the other desire I lack; desires may be individuated more finely than by a rough specification of their objects. And this is borne out by a view of desires on which they are constituted by inferential commitments: were I to discover that I could decline the gift without giving offence, I would do so; my desire does not commit me to seeking out such items in the shops myself, in the way that the desire I wish I had would. The different packages of inferential commitments make up different desires, and I can all too easily have one without possessing the other.[11]

---

10. One might be inclined to draw the terminological lines a little differently, and insist that one has the desire until one notices its provenance. Settling the question would be a matter of becoming clear about whether I have the relevant inferential commitments, which I then lose, or whether I am shown not to have them when I prove unwilling to acknowledge them. Since the present argument doesn't require settling the question, I'm going to leave it open.

11. In saying this, I don't mean to be making a reductionist claim—that is, I don't mean to suggest that one can eliminate talk of desires in favor of specified packages of inferential commitments. I am also not claiming that two desires must involve precisely the same inferential commitments in order to be counted as being the same desire. I take desire ascriptions to be a coarse grid laid over one's practical inferential commitments, and this coarseness allows room for variation. Within bounds, one can intelligibly speak of a desire's growing stronger or weaker, or of the content of a desire being made more precise.

We can now apply this general point about individuating desires to the objection at hand. We imagined the desires *strong enough* to make spending this amount of money to satisfy them positively a bargain. So even if we grant the objection's claims about what I would do if I had cash to burn, the desire must in any case be mysteriously and dramatically weakened by my knowledge that it is pill-induced. But the attributed 'strength' of a desire is a partial characterization of its inferential role, a crude way of summarizing what desires it overrides, i.e., what other inferences it preempts. The weakening of the desire is a striking change in the inferential commitments that constitute it; different inferential commitments, when the difference is as striking as this, mean different desires. When I figure out what inferential commitments I *do* have, it turns out that the pill has not managed to induce the desire it was supposed to. Notice that it would be a mistake to think that the requisite desire was induced, but overridden; since the desire was specified to be strong enough not to be overridden by the countervailing desires at work in the example, it turns out not to have been induced at all. Desiring 'at pill' did not work as promised.

The pill-induced inferential commitments are not only significantly weaker, but differ in kind from those of the desire I meant to induce. Suppose that money *were* no object. In that case I might well buy the car, just because it's easier than resisting the peculiar craving with which I am now afflicted. But I shall be unable to suppress the thought that I am doing something a little bit crazy, catering to an urge of this provenance.

Urges and desires are very different kettles of string. I am not claiming that pills cannot produce urges, any more than I would claim that pills cannot produce hallucinations. (Beliefs and hallucinations are also very different things.) I can act to assuage an urge in a manner roughly similar to that in which I might step around a small pink elephant; I do not *believe* that I am really seeing a pink elephant, but it is easier than walking through it. If I buy the Ferrett after all, the inferences that take me from the pill-induced impulse to the purchase will exhibit just this kind of indirection, which normal action or inference from a desire for the vehicle would not. Satisfying an urge as a way of preventing it from continually intruding itself into my life is not at all the same thing as pursuing a desire that shares the urge's object.

The apparent weakening and the indirection introduced into my inferences show that the alleged desire is not playing its normal inferential role. But since a desire is constituted by its inferential role, that is just to say that I do not have *that* desire. Desire-inducing pills do not induce the desires they purport to induce; at best, they provide occasion for desires to manage the urges they do induce.

§ 2.3

Although I am claiming that one cannot *just* 'desire at pill', I do not mean to insist that indirect means of acquiring desires can never be effective. Rather, I want to establish that they can be effective only if one of a class of related conditions is met.

Recall the analogous case, that of believing at will. If you remember that the only reason you believe you spent your vacation on Mars was that you visited a cut-rate travel agency that specializes in selling belief-inducing pills rather than expensive vacations, you will not actually manage to retain the belief. But if you do not remember this, there is no reason why the pill should not be effective.[12] A belief pill could be made to work if one of its side-effects was to make you forget that you had used it.

Impairing one's memory is not the only way to render such a pill effective. One might acquire a belief by taking a pill, but then come to think that, since acquiring the belief, one had come across good evidence for it. Or one could come to regard the pill as a technique of belief acquisition that gives one good reason to have a belief. (Perhaps a side-effect of the pill is to induce the belief that pills are reliable methods of belief acquisition; or perhaps one recalls having taken the pill from a friend's medicine cabinet, from the shelf labeled 'True Belief Pills'.) In cases of this kind, we have no reason to suppose that indirect methods of belief acquisition must be ineffective.[13]

---

12. The example is from Dick, 1990. To be sure, in Dick's story vacations on Mars are routine for the wealthy; in the actual world, one might come to doubt one's 'memory' on noticing that no one else seemed to be vacationing on Mars.

13. Cook, 1987, discusses a case that resembles these in its structural features.

Then again, it is apparently the realization that the way in which the belief was acquired gives one no reason to take it to be *true* that undermines the would-be belief. If that realization fails to take place, perhaps because the pill itself somehow impairs one's cognitive faculties, the pill's effectiveness need not be impugned. This possibility is related to the traditionally puzzling phenomenon of self-deception; agents are apparently sometimes able to suppress the undermining realization, although typically their behavior leads us to an equivocal judgment as to whether they have the belief under consideration or not. Both the simple failure to realize the implications of one's method of belief acquisition and the more baroque attitudes of self-deception fall under the heading of abridgments of the believer's rationality.

Lastly for now, there are the cases of self-fulfilling beliefs. Faced with the realization that, if I think I can jump it, I can jump it, some agents are able to adopt the belief that they *can* jump it. (Following James, we can call the enabling characteristic 'the will to believe'.)[14] Not surprisingly, there need be no tendency for such beliefs to be undercut by one's awareness of the way in which they were acquired, since one also realizes that, given that one *has* the belief, it is (probably) true.

There are perhaps other conditions which, if met, would permit indirect techniques for the acquisition of belief to be effective; to complete the catalog is not part of the present task. Two points deserve notice, however. One is that there is a common thread running through most of these conditions, that of the failure of a cognitive process which under normal circumstances would lead the agent to the conclusion that he has no *reason* to accept the belief in question. The second is that these conditions have rough analogs in the domain of the indirect acquisition of desires. Let me pause a moment to support this last claim.

Recall my brief career as a Honda salesman, and the subsequent failure of my would-be desire for the Honda options package. If I had simply forgotten the source of that would-be desire, it might well have

---

14. James, 1896/1961. Although it is not clear that James himself restricts the scope of the will to believe in this way, his clearest and most plausible examples are beliefs that are either self-fulfilling, or likely to seem to the agent to be self-fulfilling. This feature is shared by the examples found in the so-called 'ethics of belief' literature. Cf., e.g., Meiland, 1980.

played something very much like its customary inferential role. If I had not *forgotten,* but its relevance had somehow slipped my mind—whether merely as an oversight, or in some more complicated way—the desire would have remained intact.

Similarly, perhaps I take myself to have acquired, since taking the pill, good reasons for thinking the Ferrett options package highly desirable. Perhaps I now regard the pill as having induced a proper appreciation of the hitherto unnoticed merits of rotating hood ornaments. In neither of these cases must we suppose the pill to be ineffective.

Then again, had I somehow managed to deceive myself as to the origin of my orectic state, it might have turned out to be a full-fledged desire after all—although, as I have remarked, the behavior of the self-deceived rarely allows uncomplicated or unqualified ascription of the attitudes involved in the deception. And self-fulfilling belief has an analog as well, which I will discuss below.

As before, the list is not exhaustive. But there is nonetheless a common thread; most of the items on it are impediments to a realization. I have not yet said what that realization is, but notice the implications of the fact that it is a *realization* for the contingency of our inability to desire at will—or 'at pill'. If what the agent is realizing, when the technique fails, or what the agent is prevented from realizing, when it succeeds, is that some condition on the rational acceptability of his desire has not been met, then it is not simply an accident—and not merely an empirical fact—that one cannot decide to desire.

§ 2.4

Having established the rough outlines of the phenomenon to be explained, we can now begin to think about what might account for it. Consider the clarification that Williams gives of the impossibility of believing at will (and of the restrictions imposed on the indirect acquisition of belief) in terms of the intimate connection between belief and truth. On his view,

> it seems that we have some rather good reasons for saying that there is not much room for deciding to believe . . . it is not a contingent fact that I cannot bring it about, just like that, that I believe something . . .

Why is this? One reason is connected with the characteristic of beliefs that they aim at truth. If I could acquire a belief at will, I could acquire it whether it was true or not; moreover I would know that I could acquire it whether it was true or not . . . At the very least, there must be a restriction on what is the case after the event . . . With regard to no belief could I know—or, if all this is to be done in full consciousness, even suspect—that I had acquired it at will. But if I can acquire beliefs at will, I must know that I am able to do this.[15]

It is the realization that one has no reason to think one's belief true, and every reason to think it untrue, that undoes the belief. Can a similar explanation be given for our inability to desire at will? Claiming that desires aim at truth will not do, since desires are at any rate not directed toward truth in the same way that beliefs are. Perhaps desires are oriented toward a practical analog of truth: the Good, or the Desirable.[16] (Anscombe has pointed out that desire ascriptions fail when we cannot attribute to the agent an appropriate 'desirability characterization'.)[17] Let us suppose for the moment that this is the case.[18]

The danger with would-be explanations of this kind is that they are likely to turn out to be nonexplanatory. Truth may be the *formal* object

---

15. Williams, 1973a, pp. 147f.

16. Satisfaction is sometimes advanced as an orectic analog of truth, but as we will see, satisfaction does not explain our inability to desire at will.

17. Anscombe, 1985, sec. 38.

18. As a matter of fact, this supposition would have to be complicated considerably if it were to be used as anything more than a placeholder. 'Desirable', as the term is ordinarily used, is the orectic analog, not of 'true', but (not surprisingly, given the construction of the word) of 'believable'. We are here looking for a label for the formal object of desire, and there are many ways in which this formal object would have to differ from what we ordinarily call the desirable. For example, while I may be satisfied that Guide Michelin's criteria for a desirable restaurant are my own, when I come upon Michelin's list of twelve thousand desirable European restaurants, I do not thereby find myself with desires to eat in each of them. (Compare my response to the Guide Michelin with, first, my response to a book of (I think) *true* statements (why *not* believe them all?); and, second, to a book of *believable* statements.) And this is not a contingent fact: desires occupy a particular role in practical inference; you appeal to your desires in figuring out what to do. If one were to desire everything that one thought desirable (in the broad sense of 'desirable' in

of belief, but one cannot, in practice, appeal to the truth of a belief to explain (in the first instance, at any rate) one's maintaining it. 'I believe it because it's *true*' is mere table-thumping.

One cannot simply check one's beliefs directly against the truth; rather, one considers evidence: other beliefs one has which support or contradict it, for example, or one's observations. In short, one considers one's reasons for and against the belief. Likewise with regard to judgments of desirability, if desirability is in fact the formal object of desire. To insist that an object of desire is *desirable* is just table-thumping. In practice, one adduces one's reasons for and against thinking the object of desire desirable. The appeal to desirability, like the appeal to truth, says nothing as to why an agent does (or, in the cases we are considering, is unable to) maintain a belief or a desire. What does the work in supporting and explaining someone's belief or desire is not its truth or desirability, but the reasons for it.

Evidently, then, we should look to the considerations that bring one to adopt and sustain one's beliefs and desires for the explanation we are seeking. It may help at this point to glance over our shoulders at an earlier discussion of formal reconstructions of reasoning. Back in the heyday of analytic philosophy, A. N. Prior argued against the view that a logical operator could be specified by an arbitrary list of 'introduction rules' and 'elimination rules'. To show the absurdity of this view, Prior defined an operator he called 'tonk', which was to share its introduction rule with 'or' and its elimination rule with 'and'. That is, from p, it would be legitimate to infer p-tonk-q (just as from p one may infer p-or-q), and from p-tonk-q it would be legitimate to infer q (just as from p-and-q one may infer q). Were one permitted to use an operator like tonk in one's inferences, one would be able to infer any conclusion from any premise whatsover. Clearly, such a 'logical operator' has no place in reasoning

---

which the twelve thousand restaurants in the Guide Michelin are desirable), one's 'desires' would be unable to play that role.

For this reason, among others, in giving the formal object of desire the label 'desirability', we must not suppose that we have yet said what the bearer of the label is, or what it looks like.

(which is to say, there is no reason to call it 'logical'); one cannot pair just any introduction rules with just any elimination rules. Introduction and elimination rules must be carefully matched, so as to permit the latter to be applied only when it would be acceptable to apply them.[19]

Now there is a similar point to be made with regard to the psychological states that constitute thought. There is, on the one hand, the range of conclusions that one is permitted and committed to draw from one's belief or desire (against the relevant background of one's other beliefs and desires), and, on the other, the range of considerations that warrants one's adopting the belief or desire in question. If these are not carefully matched, tonky inference will be inevitable.

I earlier said that I took desires to be constituted by the inferential commitments involved in them. We can now distinguish between *forward-* and *backward-directed* inferential commitments. Forward-directed commitments are a matter of what inferences I am committed to making; for example, if I believe that *p*, I am committed, upon learning that *p* entails *q*, to inferring *q*. (This is not to say that I must live up to all my commitments. For one thing, I may find myself overcommitted—as when I am committed to inferring, from other premises, not-*q*. In these cases, I may retrench, abandoning my belief that *p*.) Backward-directed commitments, on the other hand, are a matter of the origin and reasonableness of the psychological states from which my inferences are going to proceed; the examples discussed by Williams and his commentators show, roughly, that if I believe that *p* I am committed to having arrived at and having maintained my belief in ways that have a suitable amount to do with its truth—or, recalling that the appeal to truth is unhelpful, in ways that underwrite the inferences I am committed to drawing in virtue of having the belief.[20]

---

19. Prior, 1960. Michael Dummett draws a very similar moral from tonk and its relatives (1973, pp. 396f); I'm grateful to Lloyd Humberstone for directing me to Dummett's discussion.

20. While skepticism exploits the fact that we have these commitments, I do not think it obvious that our backward-directed inferential commitments require me to be able to adduce evidence in support of all my beliefs, or surrender them—that is, I am not providing a quick argument for skepticism. I believe my address to be 2143 Rose Street, so I am committed, roughly, to having arrived at this belief in a satisfactory manner. But

My forward-directed commitments must be matched to my backward-directed inferential commitments, if mental activity is to amount to thought.[21] This is no less true of desires than of beliefs; if we pick out mental states as beliefs and desires by the roles they play in thought, then those roles must be such as to make thought possible. Since desires serve as a basis for practical inference, desires must involve backward-directed commitments, commitments to the effect, roughly, that the desire was acquired and sustained in ways that support the practical inferences to be made from it. (I won't yet try to say what reasons for acquiring and sustaining a desire might look like; but if this explanation of our inability to desire at will is correct, then just having wanted the desire is not normally among them.) When one becomes aware that those commitments cannot be met, desire, like belief, is undermined.

Consider an agent whose desires are uniformly tonky: this would be, for all practical purposes, an agent who acquired and lost desires entirely randomly. If this agent were to take its tonky desires seriously, as bases for practical inference, there would soon not be much agency to the alleged agent: planning, projects, and continuity would all be rendered impossible. If an agent with many tonky desires is not simply to disintegrate, it must come to regard these putative desires, whatever their phenomenological coloring, as alien intrusions upon its mind, not to be taken account of in practical inference (except as obstacles to be

---

for the life of me I could not say how I did arrive at this belief—and this fact does not impugn the commitment, for I am sure that I *did* arrive at the belief in a suitable fashion.

There is of course a similar point to be made about desires; I may hold on to a desire even though I cannot say how the backward-directed inferential commitments involved in it are met, as long as I take it that they *are* met.

21. The contrast I have just invoked, between thought and mere mental activity, might be made out in terms of a favored theory of rationality. But then of course that contrast would give us no leverage in choosing among theories of practical rationality, which is what we are now trying to do. I mean instead to be drawing on a relatively independent notion of coherent agency, on the supposition, expressed by the dated-sounding description of Logic as the Laws of Thought, that the right way to figure out what it takes to be rational is to figure out what it takes to have a mind, and consequently that the right way to figure out what it takes to be practically rational is to figure out what it takes to be an agent. (I do not, however, mean to suggest that *everything* that is needed for intelligent agency to come about belongs in one's theory of rationality.)

attended to and coped with). To the extent that an agent's desires are tonky, agency falters; to the extent that agency resists, the supposed desires are not in fact desires.

Tonky would-be desires further impair agency by precluding practical reasoning. To anticipate the arguments of the next chapter, practical inference includes at least the form of reasoning that gets discussed under the heading of the practical syllogism. Practical syllogisms are defeasible, and mastery and deployment of this form of inference requires exhibiting sensitivity to defeating conditions. Now such sensitivity in turn requires that the reasoner understand *why* the respective considerations matter. (It is a mistake to assume that such deliberations must turn on *how much* the respective considerations matter; in a large and important class of cases, the quantitative judgment appears only as a retrospective summary of the result of the deliberation.) But in the case of tonky 'desires' one is unable to say why the 'desire' or its object matters. (Another way of putting this is to say that one becomes unable to give a desirability characterization that makes sense—which, as remarked above, prevents ascription of the desire.) So tonky would-be desires undercut mastery of inferential apparatus we cannot do without. If we are to think with our propositional attitudes, they must involve backward-directed commitments that are appropriate to their forward-directed commitments.

§ 2.5

Desires, then, involve backward-directed inferential commitments. Backward-directed commitments provide a unified explanation for our initially ad hoc list of restrictions on the acquisition of beliefs and desires at will and 'at pill'. Since I am concerned here with deciding to desire, I will leave the verification of this claim as it pertains to beliefs as an exercise for the reader, and will proceed directly to the restrictions we have surveyed on the acquisition of desires.

The range of cases in which one cannot desire at will—and the correlative range of cases in which one cannot desire 'at pill'—may be explained in terms of the account we have been developing as follows. An agent who is aware that his desires have been acquired at will or 'at pill' has no reason to suppose that the backward-directed commitments involved in his desires can be met, and every reason to suppose they cannot. But it is his ability to suppose that these commitments are met that allows him the forward-directed inferential commitments involved in his desire. And absent these—that is, when the agent is no longer willing to undertake the practical inferences that proceed from the desire—the conditions for ascribing the desire itself are no longer met.

The conditions that permit deciding to desire prove to be, not items on an ad hoc list, but principled consequences of the explanation I have proposed. If the agent fails to realize that his backward-directed commitments cannot be met, his willingness to follow through on his forward-directed commitments will remain unimpaired; realization may be forestalled by forgetfulness, inattentiveness, self-deception, or other, more exotic means. Conversely, if those commitments are met despite the non-standard method through which the desire was acquired—or, more precisely, if the agent *takes* them to be met—then, again, he will stand by his forward-directed commitments. The agent may take himself to have good reasons for desiring what he does that are unconnected with the way in which he acquired the desire; or he may confusedly think that the non-standard method tracks good reasons; or he may be aware that, in *this* case, the non-standard method *does* track good reasons.[22]

If my explanation of the restrictions on our ability to desire at will or 'at pill' is correct, it follows that deciding to desire is impossible, *except* when some condition derivable from the explanation is met—examples being the items on our short working list. There are a number of further exceptions to the claim that one cannot desire 'at pill'; we are now ready to consider three more of them. (Once again, the list of exceptions is by no means exhaustive; when the general principle that generates them is understood, particular cases are worth examining only when there's something to be learned from them.)

The first of these is that frequently encountered inhabitant of philosophical thought experiments, the addict. The addict seems to be an

---

22. Sometimes, our desires do not fall into line by themselves, and we take steps to bring them into line. The self-destructive neurotic who enters psychotherapy, the shy person at the party who drinks in order to build up his self-confidence, and the chronically depressed individual who turns to Prozac are examples. When these steps are effective, a crucial ingredient is normally the idea that the desires one is bringing oneself to have are those one should have had anyway—that is, that one is bringing oneself to have desires whose backward-directed commitments are met.

unfortunately commonplace instance of an agent who has acquired a desire 'at pill', is aware that he has done so, is aware that the object of the desire is in fact entirely undesirable, yet nonetheless engages in practical inference proceeding from the desire. That is, addiction is an apparent counterexample to the unified account we have been developing of the inability to desire at will.

Now the philosopher's addict is in reality not nearly as commonplace as is often supposed; much addiction is far less straightforward than the description just given allows. For one thing, the desire may be complex in ways that obscure the agent's view of its merely chemical source; in nicotine addicts, for example, elements of ritual, attention to self-image, the tactics of social intercourse, the use of a cigarette to relax, or to focus one's mind, or to pretend that one is not simply sitting all alone by oneself in a public place—all these may seem to the agent to underwrite the desire for a smoke, rather than being merely produced by it. (And perhaps some of them *do* underwrite the desire to smoke.) For another, self-deception may be involved: I can stop whenever I want; just one more won't hurt; the medical evidence is disputed; it 'separates the men from the boys (but not from the girls)'; it's a badge of gender equality ('you've come a long way, baby'). That self-deception is so common in cases of addiction supports the view I am developing. It is because it is essential that the backward-directed commitments involved in a desire be met that addicts so often engage in the mental contortions that allow them to imagine that they can be. Then again, an addict may take his feelings as an indication that his desires are in order. (This is often perfectly legitimate; we will return to this point in Chapter 6.) And finally, an addict may simply lose sight of other things that matter to him.[23]

If I am right, then, clear-headed addicts are far less common than one might have supposed. I do not mean to insist, however, that such addicts do not exist. How can I account for any who do? Consider the epistemic analog: it might have been thought that the argument due to Williams shows that a clear-headed consumer of hallucinogens cannot

---

23. This last point is due to Alyssa Bernstein.

actually come to have the beliefs his drugs seem to induce. But perhaps the hallucination is so vivid, so immediate, that even though one *knows* that the three-headed Elvis is an effect of the drug, one cannot help shaking his hand. I do not mean to deny that this can happen; I do think that if we bring such a person's inferential commitments into tight focus, we shall have to say something a good deal more complicated than that he believes he is confronting a three-headed Elvis.

I propose to use cases of this kind as a model for understanding the clear-headed addict. Earlier I distinguished urges from desires, and suggested an analogy between urges and hallucinations. Perhaps some urges cannot be ignored, in roughly the way that some hallucinations cannot be ignored; again, however, bringing the inferential commitments of the clear-headed addict overcome by his drug-induced urge into tight focus will require us to say something more complicated than: he desires the drug. If this way of understanding the addict proves generally applicable, he will not in fact be a counterexample to the claim that, modulo the specified conditions, one cannot desire 'at pill', but will rather be an instance of inducing pharmaceutically a state that is not desire, but is related to it.

The addict may seem sufficiently extreme to be exceptional. After all, need it be the case that trivial preferences (e.g., for one flavor of ice cream over another) are undermined by the knowledge that they were pill-induced? Reminded that my preference for chocolate over vanilla is due solely to the chemical effects of previously consumed chocolate, I may shrug and order the chocolate anyway. But this kind of case also conforms to the general principle for which I have been arguing. My backward-directed inferential commitments must *match* my forward-directed inferential commitments, and when my forward-directed commitments do not amount to much, my backward-directed commitments need not amount to much either. Nothing is at stake in my choice of flavor; it really does not matter what I choose. In such a case, 'I just feel like it' is a good enough reason—even though it is no reason at all, but a rejection of the demand for a reason.[24] Here desire verges on whim.

---

24. Once again, the point is Anscombe's (1985, sec. 39).

Of course, the desire for chocolate ice cream may well not be whim; normally, my reason for ordering it is the way I expect it to taste. (This is why, even in this relatively trivial case, I cannot simply *decide* to want a different flavor of ice cream—though I can decide to try it a few times in the hope of learning to like it.) And this observation gives us a way of explaining some of the apparently unsupported preferences that are not at all trivial. One's sexuality may determine much of the shape of one's life, even if one believes that it is just one's hormones at work, or that one is being the cat's-paw of Darwinian evolution. Why don't such beliefs undercut one's willingness to make life-shaping decisions on the basis of the desires that (in large part) constitute one's sexuality? Of course, they may; but when they do not, it is because such desires seem to the agent to be supported: someone who professes, say, a particular sexual orientation presumably enjoys sex with individuals of the specified gender, finds some of them attractive, and so on; and if not, we may suspect that life-shaping decisions on the basis of the desires involved in that sexual orientation are at least hasty.

We can say that many desires are supported by our *tastes*. This raises the following possibility: that while we cannot expect desire-producing pills to work directly, they could be effective if they worked indirectly, that is, if they altered one's tastes. If the range of tastes that can be induced is broad enough, then, in practice, there will be a quite wide range of desires that could, in principle, be acquired at will.[25]

I will defer the question of whether (and which) tastes can be modified at will, or 'at pill', to Chapter 6. Once we understand what judgments of taste amount to, and the role they play in cognition, it will turn out that there are also—and not coincidentally—rather severe restrictions on modifying tastes at will, or 'at pill'.

§ 2.6

Some time back, I mentioned that self-fulfilling beliefs were an occasional exception to the dictum that one cannot believe at will. I now want to examine an orectic analog of this phenomenon. Consider the

---

25. I'm grateful to Sydney Shoemaker (1997) for pressing me on this point.

role that might be played by one's theory of desirability (or of the Good) in determining the stability of a pill-induced desire. If one's theory of desirability were such that one had no reason to think that, in general, the object of a pill-induced desire must be desirable, then reflection on the fact that one has the desire only because one has taken a pill would tend to undermine the desire. But suppose that one's theory of desirability were: what it is for x to be desirable is just for x to be desired. (Call this theory the 'desirability = desired theory', or DDT.) Then on taking the pill, one will find the objects of one's pill-induced desire to be desirable; and in that case, we have seen no reason to think that they will prove unstable. Apparently, a theory of desirability can produce exceptions to the general claim that one cannot 'desire at pill'; if a theory like DDT is correct, and comes to be understood to be correct, the claim that one cannot 'desire at pill' will fall by the wayside, the exception having become the general case.

One response to this difficulty might be to argue that the theory of desirability is *crazy*. Consider the analogous objection to the analogous claim about belief. Pragmatism says that truth is what would be believed at the limit of inquiry; call 'complacent pragmatism' the view that takes the limit of inquiry to be the present moment: truth is what I believe now.[26] The complacent pragmatist's pill-induced beliefs need not be epistemically unstable, because he has no reason to think that his pill-induced beliefs do not track the truth. The correct response to this objection would be that the complacent pragmatist theory of truth is just crazy; one is irrational if one's pill-induced beliefs are stable for this reason, because one is irrational in accepting the complacent pragmatist theory of truth. Why not use the same response to the DDT-based objection?

Here I want, once again, to run the argument in the other direction. If DDT, or some close relative of it, were understood to be true, 'desiring at pill' would be possible across the board; moreover, I will argue in a moment that desiring at will would be possible across the board as well. Since neither of these *are* possible across the board, this shows that nobody, not even those who espouse DDT-like views, actually takes

---

26. I'm grateful to Henry Richardson for the label for this view.

them seriously enough to reason in accordance with them. And this goes a long way toward demonstrating the implausibility of such views.

Recall James on the will to believe: James defends "faith running ahead of scientific evidence" in cases "where faith in a fact can help create the fact."[27] While I am uncertain that his own examples support the contention he is often read as making (roughly, that when certain questions cannot be answered, you may believe what you like), I think that they, and examples like them, show that self-fulfilling beliefs are something of an exception to the general dictum that one cannot believe at will. (This does not make them an exception to the underlying explanation, that one can believe things only if one takes one's beliefs to be responsive to the truth of the beliefs, and it does not make them an exception to the claim that beliefs acquired in a way that gives you no reason to think their objects true are epistemically unstable. Self-fulfilling beliefs are acquired in a way that gives you reason to think their objects true.) To be sure, not everybody can do this; but there is a character trait or attitude toward the world—'the will to believe'—that allows one to say: 'If I believe I can jump it, I can jump it; alright, I can jump it.'

Now the analog of a self-fulfilling belief is a self-endorsing desire, a desire whose object is desirable provided one desires it. Some things really are like this; although in most cases, desirability that depends on desire (marriages, for example, are only desirable if the participants desire them) depends also on much else (desire alone does not a happy or worthwhile marriage make). And there are people, I think, who, in these rare cases, are able to make the transition paralleling that of the will to believe: 'If I wanted it, it would be worth wanting; I want it.'[28] We can call the attitude that characterizes such people 'the will to desire'.

According to DDT, *all* objects of desire are desirable provided one desires them, and all desires are self-endorsing. So the realization that DDT has this entailment will be enough to keep the desire of an agent persuaded of DDT stable in the face of contemplating its acquisition by

---

27. James, 1896/1961, p. 105, italics deleted.

28. For example, perhaps deciding to root for a team (which involves wanting that team to win) is possible because the desirability of the team's winning is exhausted by one's attitude toward it. (The example comes from Harman, 1976.)

a pill; if DDT were true, then 'desiring at pill' would be possible across the board, and we have argued that it is not. Still, this latter claim may be regarded as controversial; the advocate of DDT may respond that we have only shown 'desiring at pill' to be impossible provided one has a mistaken theory of desirability.

But if belief in DDT were enough to make 'desiring at pill' possible, it would be enough, provided the agent had 'the will to desire', to effect the transition from wanting to have the desire to having the desire. Observation indicates that, while not everyone has the will to desire, there are quite enough people who do, enough of whom, in turn, profess a DDT-like theory of practical reasoning. (I'll return to that theory in just a moment.) Let me acknowledge that it is an empirical premise of my argument that there are people whose characters make them a litmus test for the possibility of desiring at will; that premise granted, recall that it is a flat fact that one cannot, across the board, desire at will. So, first, the DDT-based objection to the argument against 'desiring at pill' fails. And second, I take it that the explanation for the failure is that nobody really believes DDT, or anything like it—that is, whatever they *say*, they don't believe it deeply enough to engage in practical reasoning as though it were true. This is why those individuals with the will to desire are able to exercise it only in those rare cases where they are able to see that the desirability does depend on their desiring.

§ 2.7

We have established that (modulo qualifications which I will not now repeat) wanting to have a particular desire will not bring one to have it, and that this is not merely an empirical fact. On our way to establishing this thesis we have seen that views that are committed to desires being, *qua* desires, self-justifying, are untenable; the foremost such view is of course instrumentalism, which holds that all practical reasoning, and consequently all practical justification, is instrumental, or means-end. Instrumental reasoning bottoms out in desires that are not themselves instrumentally justified, and if instrumental reasoning is all the practical reasoning there is, simply having such desires must be enough to underwrite practical inferences from them. But practical inference on the basis

of whatever desires one happens to have is on a par with tonky 'inference'; and for thought of any kind, and practical inference in particular,
to be possible, inference must not be tonky. Appreciation of this fact
is exhibited in our inferential practice—and it is even exhibited in the
practice of those who pay lip-service to instrumentalism. No one actually reasons as though instrumentalism were true.

I need to say a word or two about the propriety of assimilating instrumentalist to tonky 'inference'. After all, it might seem that instrumentalist agency is not as badly off as tonky would-be agency, because
most of us possess a relatively stable and manageable set of desires, and
because those desires do exercise control over our practical inferences in
a way that the states of mind from which tonky mental activity proceeds do not. However, that our desires are by and large manageable is,
from the point of view of the instrumentalist conception of rationality, a
lucky accident, and so not a fact to which the instrumentalist can appeal.
While desires, on the instrumentalist account, exercise control over inferences downstream, nothing upstream exercises control over the initial
desires: when it comes to these, anything goes. Tonk permits the inferential move from any p to any q in two steps; instrumentalism permits the
move to any desire in just one step, that of coming to have the desire. If
we are unified and coherent agents nonetheless, that is because our good
luck is not actually *luck* at all: our desires are manageable because we are
not instrumentalist reasoners.

If the force of this point is insufficiently appreciated, I suspect that is
because there seems to be a way for the instrumentalist to insure that
manageable sets of desires are more than just fortunate coincidences.
Second-order desires, that is, desires that take other desires as their objects, have enjoyed a recent popularity as an available and effective device
that can be used in the philosophical analysis of agency, persons, and values, as well as practical reasoning.[29] And second-order desires can serve

---

29. See, e.g., Frankfurt, 1988, Jeffrey, 1974, Lewis, 1989. For a dissenting view, see Harman, 1993. I myself doubt that appeal to second-order desires is usually philosophically
helpful, and I believe that the claims for which I have been arguing can help to show
that, perhaps with rare exceptions, second-order desires cannot do the jobs they have
been asked to do. But that is a topic for another time and place.

to make instrumentalism seem more plausible than it would otherwise appear.

Consider an instrumental justification: goal A is justified by showing it to be a means to goal B, which is in turn justified by showing it to be a means to goal C. . . If circularity and regress are to be avoided, one's justification bottoms out in ends that one just *has;* these ends are beyond the purview of rational assessment, or so it seems.[30] Now the apparent arbitrariness of one's ultimate ends can seem objectionable—both undesirable, and untrue to our own critical practices. For example, it is sometimes claimed that intransitive preferences are irrational because an agent who has them can be turned into a money pump.[31] One might similarly criticize a friend for sticking to desires that are bound to be frustrated. And one might regard a tonky 'agent'—one who acquired and

---

30. Circularity can be defended in the context of coherence theories of practical justification. But experiment shows that coherentist inference, even when the only connections under consideration are those allowable by instrumentalism, produces results that are incompatible with instrumentalism. See Millgram and Thagard, 1996.

Let me say a word or two about what coherentist accounts of practical reasoning look like against the argument I have been developing. If a desire's cohering with other desires is thought of as an inferential relation, then coherentism survives the argument against instrumentalism: on such a view, the backward-directed inferential commitments involved in a desire have to do with that desire's cohering with other desires (and, presumably, beliefs); as in other cases, discovering that you have no reason to think that one of your desires does cohere with the rest will undercut it. That it does survive is bound up with the ways in which adjustments to one's orectic system, and actions stemming from it, can, even when always justified in terms of one's desires, fail to be driven by their *satisfaction.* This leaves a terminological confusion to be cleared up. I sometimes speak of instrumentalism as tantamount to the view that practical reasoning bottoms out in one's desires, but this might leave one wondering whether a coherentist position couched in terms of desires would count as a form of instrumentalism, on my view. (I'm grateful to Henry Richardson for pressing me on this point.) Talk of 'bottoming out' in desires should be understood as meaning: appealing to the *satisfaction* of one's (present) desires.

31. Davidson et al., 1955, p. 146. For those unfamiliar with the argument, here is the gist of it: Suppose you prefer A to B, B to C, and C to A, and suppose that you now have A and I have B and C. Then there is some price you will pay me, say, $5, in order to trade A for C. Once you have C, you will be willing to pay another $5 in order to trade C for B; and once you have B you will be ready to pay yet another $5 in order to trade B for A. Now we are back where we started—you have A and I have B and C—but you have paid $15 for the privilege, and we are ready to begin the cycle of trades once again.

lost desires frequently and at random, and so became unable to develop coherent plans for pursuing its ends—as failing to meet minimal standards of practical rationality. How can one's ultimate desires be beyond the purview of instrumental reasoning *and* be subject to the criticism that they are irrational, if instrumentalism is correct?

Second-order desires can seem to provide a way out of this difficulty. Having intransitive preferences renders one a possible victim of predatory manipulation, and we may suppose that most agents do not want to become victims of predatory manipulation. Similarly, most agents do not want to be frustrated, and they want to be able to take effective steps toward the goals they have. The agent is irrational, rather than merely unfortunate, in that he has good reason not to have those preferences— the justification being given here not in terms of the objects of those preferences, but in terms of the preferences—that is, the mental states— themselves. More generally, while the instrumental justification of one's desires must bottom out in desires whose contents do not stand in the means-end relation to the contents of further desires, the bottoming-out desires need not be reprehensibly arbitrary because, as psychological attitudes, they can be objects of judgments of desirability. What is justified are not contents of one's propositional attitudes, but the psychological envelopes they come in.[32]

Now the fact that an agent possesses unsatisfied second-order preferences or desires is not yet enough to convict him of irrationality; if he does not have the preferences he wishes he had, isn't he merely unfortunate? How can we blame an agent for being unable to satisfy his desires, if their objects (that is, his further desires) are beyond his control? Evidently there is a presumption at work here to the effect that in a rational agent second-order desires are *effective*: that when the drawbacks of his current preferences are made evident to him, the intransitively preferenced agent will, or should, adjust his preferences; that when one realizes that one's current desires are bound to be frustrated, in light of one's second-order desire not to be frustrated, one will, or should, abandon one's desires. But the thesis that one cannot decide to desire also severely

---

32. See Schmidtz, 1995, ch. 3, for a view of this kind.

restricts the philosophical uses of second-order desires: if my argument has been on-target the presumption of effectiveness is unavailable. One cannot decide to desire, and one cannot (once again, excepting the conditions I have indicated above) acquire desires or preferences through indirect methods. Second-order desires cannot account for the manageability of the desires we turn out to have.

Often, of course, one's desires are modified or abandoned when one comes to desire that they be modified or abandoned; but that is just because the normal process of coming to see a desire should be abandoned is that of coming to see the desire as a *mistake,* that is, as a desire for something that is not (in the most formal sense) desirable. All the work is being done by attention to whether the backward-directed commitments involved in the desire being dislodged are met; none, or very little, is done by the accompanying second-order desire.

§ 2.8

Instrumentalism is a mistake. It fails because it requires practical justification to bottom out in desires that themselves cannot involve further backward-directed commitments. But because desires figure in practical reasoning as bases for inference, they *must* involve backward-directed inferential commitments, and second-order desires are not an adequate substitute. If this is right, we need to explain how the backward-directed commitments involved in our desires are met; and that, with a shift in terminology, will be the topic of the next five chapters.

Why a shift in terminology? 'Desire' is a philosophers' term of art, and, as I remarked earlier, is often distinguished from belief in terms of 'direction of fit': beliefs are adjusted to fit the world, as opposed to desires, to which features of the world are, with greater or lesser success, adjusted. That is, philosophers ordinarily arrive at the notion of desire by combining two ideas. The first is that of a mental state that serves as a basis for practical inference: you act so as to make the world conform to your desires. (This was how we introduced the notion of desire at the outset of the chapter.) The second is the idea of a mental state not involving backward-directed inferential commitments. (Even when some desires are grounded in other desires, eventually one comes around to desires that one just *has*.) What we have seen is that this combination is unworkable; in a rational and unified agent, there is nothing corresponding to this combination of ideas—or, at any rate, there are not enough of such items to matter. A dramatic way to put this conclusion might be to say that it has turned out that desires, as construed by the philosophical tradition, do not exist.[33]

If the word, in its technical philosophical sense, lacks occasions for use, it might be withdrawn from circulation, so as to make it less likely to interfere with its plain English homonym, a very interesting (and, now and then, useful) word denoting a felt state closely related to craving and lust. Because there is philosophical capital built up by instrumentalism's long appropriation of the word, I will continue, now and again, to talk of desires; when I do, I will mean by the word psychological states (or, indifferently, those aspects of psychological states) that involve a motive for, and are taken as providing a reason for, bringing about their objects. Calling a state a desire will not imply that there is no more to it than that—that it is something one can take oneself to 'just have'—though it may be used to emphasize the fact that instrumentalists see the state in this light.

---

33. Michael Bratman has recently argued that intentions are central to agency because they provide the stability needed for developing plans in stages and for coordinating plans belonging to more than one person (1987). The important feature of an intention is that, having formed one, one keeps it until one has reason to reconsider and reject it. And this might suggest that even if one cannot *desire* at will, one can *intend* at will: intentions, after all, ought to be resistant to the kind of second thoughts that I have been claiming undercut unsupported desires.

Gregory Kavka has pointed out that one can no more intend at will than one can decide to desire (1983); I think that the explanation of this fact is the one we have already given. However, there remains a genuine issue here that I want to flag for future attention. Intentions do plausibly take up some of the slack that appears when practical conclusions are underdetermined by the reasons for them. An example of Bratman's makes the point nicely: I could take either of two highways to San Francisco, and there is really nothing to be said for one over the other. When I decide which to take, my awareness that I did not have sufficient reason to take that route does not necessarily undermine my determination to take it. I decide, and that's that. Since very little of our practical reasoning is deductive, we can expect underdetermination of one kind or another to be quite frequent. If this is right, we need to consider how, and how much of, such slack can be taken up.

But my use of the term will only be occasional, since it will usually be less misleading to have a replacement on hand for our discussion of practical reasoning. We need a term denoting mental states from which practical inferences are drawn, and the term I will be using is 'practical judgment'. In the introduction, I suggested that we need a way of talking about practical inferences that keeps our options open as to what their formal and psychological elements are, on the grounds that the only way to answer those questions would be to read them off our completed theory of practical reasoning—a theory we do not yet have. By using the placeholder term 'practical judgment', we have a way of referring to the elements of practical inferences without prejudging substantive issues that it is too early to address. (The expression is meant to be indifferent between denoting mental states and the contents of those states.)

The notion of practical judgment, like other such notions, still needs to be tied to a pattern of inference; because the point of having it is to stay as flexible as possible, the inference pattern I will use is Aristotle's practical syllogism. The reason for doing so is that—if scholarly questions about Aristotle exegesis are left to one side, and perhaps even if they are not—practical syllogisms can be treated as being a very loose-fitting way of schematizing practical inferences.[34]

Practical syllogisms have major (or general) premises, minor (or particular) premises, and conclusions; they look roughly like this:

1. Delicious things should be eaten. [major premise]
2. This cake is delicious. [minor premise]
3. Eat the cake. [conclusion]

We can allow ourselves a great deal of freedom as to how we think of and represent the elements of a practical syllogism. For instance, the

---

34. Recall that Aristotle very famously insisted that one should not try for more precision than a subject matter will bear (*NE* 1094b10–15).

I want to allow that even with as loose-fitting a schema as the practical syllogism, there may be components of practical inference that this way of attaching the label 'practical judgment' does not pick out—for example, because there are general considerations that will not, without the help of other practical considerations, support even tentative practical conclusions. Nevertheless, what we have on hand will do the job we now need done.

sense of the major premise of the practical syllogism we're examining could also have been satisfactorily rendered by any of the following:

4. I like eating delicious things.
5. Eating delicious things is a good idea.
6. When something is delicious, go ahead and eat it.

. . . and so on. And the conclusion might be variously construed as a particular evaluative judgment, a command to oneself, a decision, an intention, or even an action. The point is that for present purposes we don't need to distinguish these; a practical judgment is anything that can appear as the major premise or the conclusion of a practical syllogism, and so they will all be counted as practical judgments.

Philosophical talk of desires usually comes with a built-in commitment to instrumentalism; having adopted vocabulary that does not involve a commitment to a view we have seen good reason to reject, we can proceed to consider what, besides instrumental derivation from prior desires, can underwrite our practical judgments, and so allow us to understand our practical backward-directed inferential commitments to be met.

3

Collecting Your Thoughts

I have observed a great many ravens in a great many circumstances, and they have all been black; I infer that all ravens are black. As the stock example reminds us, induction is a very familiar form of inference. Induction proceeds from instances to generalizations, and it bottoms out in experience; and while these two aspects of inductive inference occasionally come apart,[1] we are very lucky that they are so often found in tandem. Experience is always of particulars, and if we want to learn useful lessons—that is, lessons that apply to new particulars—from what we have been through, we have no alternative but to generalize from those particulars we have already encountered. Induction is the avenue along which an absolutely indispensable part of our knowledge of the world comes.

I'm going to argue that there is an analog of induction in the practical domain. We can learn what matters from experience, and we can infer more general practical judgments from more particular practical judgments that are their instances. Time and again, someone has found that traveling is not what it is cracked up to be; even when his trip goes

---

1. Sometimes inductive inference proceeds from facts that are not empirical to generalizations from them that are not empirical either: one can believe general mathematical facts, which are presumably not just empirically true, on the basis of induction from their instances, which are also not just empirically true. (Such induction is of course to be distinguished from mathematical induction, which is a different thing entirely.) For discussion of an interestingly related case, see Thagard, 1993.

entirely as planned, he is disappointed. He concludes that traveling is overrated. When I was somewhat younger, I thought that civility was not very important; but now that I have observed enough rudeness to see the difference it makes, I find that it is quite important, after all. When I do, I have learned a general fact about what matters, and I have learned it from particular experiences. I have had many cups of Peet's coffee, and each of them was not bad at all; in fact, each of them was definitely worth drinking. I conclude that Peet's coffee is worth drinking.[2] Here I have learned a fact about what is worth doing, again, by generalizing from particular experiences. I propose to call the pattern of inference in play here *practical induction*.

§ 3.1

There are a small number of preliminaries that we need to get out of the way before we can proceed to the argument proper.

The inference from 'Raven *A* is black', 'Raven *B* is black', 'Raven *C* is black', and so on, to 'All ravens are black' is something of a caricature of the way inductive inference really works. If 'induction' is a label for the way we learn general truths from experience, we will want to count, for example, a good deal of what goes under the heading of theory construction and theory choice in the sciences as induction, or as of a piece with it; but good science looks, on the face of it, very different from the enumeration of black ravens. Likewise, the inference from 'Last year's trip was disappointing', 'This year's trip was disappointing', and so on, to 'Trips are disappointing', fails to capture a good deal of how our inferences from particular practical judgments to general practical judgments proceed. This might suggest taking time out to develop an adequate account of practical induction before trying to argue for its legitimacy; after all, how can one argue for something if one doesn't have a clear picture of what one is arguing for? But I will not proceed this way, for two reasons.

---

2. This particular inference predates Peet's reincarnation as a chain. Your mileage may vary.

First, even though it is a part of our intellectual toolkit that we could not get by without, theoretical induction is not very well understood, and the amount of unsuccessful effort that has been expended on producing a satisfactory account of it suggests that it is a hard problem.[3] It's useful to proceed on the assumption that practical induction and traditional (theoretical) induction parallel each other in many respects; this suggests that formulating a full-fledged theory of practical induction may also be a task for which we are not yet prepared. If this is right, then postponing consideration of the legitimacy of practical induction until its workings have been fully mapped out would amount to postponing it indefinitely. There is no good reason to wait: if we are looking for a characterization of practical induction, parts of it are bound to emerge in the course of an inquiry into its legitimacy; and, in any case, there is likely to be more interest in mapping out the workings of practical induction if we have some reason to think that it *is* a legitimate form of inference.

In the meantime, we will have to make do with a caricature. There is nothing wrong with that—caricatures can be quite useful for some purposes—as long as we are careful to remember that it *is* a caricature. That means proceeding with caution, using our judgment as to what aspects of our representations of patterns of inference we can take seriously and what aspects we are better off disregarding; if I am right in thinking that the argument will tell us something of what practical induction has to look like, our model of practical induction will become less cartoon-like as we go. To recap what we have at hand: A practical induction proceeds from practical judgments at a relatively lower level of generality to a practical judgment at a relatively higher level of generality that subsumes the more particular practical judgments as instances.

One last point before we can get going: a common response to examples of the kind I have used to introduce practical induction is the counter-claim that what is at work in these examples is just plain old induction. Now there are two ways to take this counter-claim, only one

---

3. For a relatively recent interdisciplinary discussion, see Holland et al., 1986.

of which I have to contest. It might express the view that practical and theoretical induction are really the same inference pattern, at work in different domains of application. As I indicated in the introduction, I think it is still premature to take a stand on this question; in any case, I do not need to disagree. Someone who is committed to this view may read the arguments in this chapter as directed toward the conclusion that induction has a genuinely practical domain of application.

However, the counter-claim might instead express the view that there is nothing going on in examples like these but specifically theoretical induction. This I do need to contest, and I will argue against it in section 5.4, when my response can be presented as the corollary of more general conclusions. But that's a long way away, and keeping the objection on hold until then may seem like a lot to ask. So let me explain why the objection is less urgent than it looks.

To see what the suggestion amounts to, consider a practical induction whose conclusion is that, at the end of a long day, there's nothing like hot polenta. (This conclusion is to be understood as a *practical* judgment: at the end of the long day, I act on it by making and eating polenta baked with artichokes and tomatoes.)[4] The objection has it that whatever induction is to be found in this reasoning must be specifically theoretical induction: I have discovered, inductively, some general fact about how hot polenta tastes or about how I react to it. The practical aspect of my

---

4. Somerville, 1993, p. 207. Recall from section 2.8 that a practical judgment is one able to serve as the major premise or conclusion of a practical syllogism.

It's worth mentioning how our makeshift criterion rules out one variation of the objection: that the induction is theoretical because it terminates in an evaluative, but not practical, conclusion. (Here, an evaluation of hot polenta.) If, as I earlier claimed, such evaluative sentences serve to express the major premises of practical syllogisms, then they express practical judgments. The inclination to think otherwise deserves diagnosis; our grip on the contents of such judgments is loose enough to suggest that the insistence on imposing these distinctions is theory-driven. The theory in question is almost certainly instrumentalism, with its insistence on sorting mental states into beliefs and desires. (If being assertable is thought to require being a belief, and if being a belief precludes being motivating, then anything that could be the conclusion of an argument must not, until a further desire is added, have practical import; and so a category—'evaluative belief'— must be created for items of this kind.) If the diagnosis is correct, and if the argument of Chapter 2 has been accepted, then we can dismiss this version of the objection as depending on a distinction we have neither reason nor means to make.

conclusion is a subsequent addition—perhaps the desire, at the end of a long day, to eat something that tastes this way.

Now of course such reconstructions are sometimes correct. The counter-claim is a problem because it insists that such an analysis of apparent instances of practical induction is always possible, and that therefore there is not *really* any practical induction at all. But this strongly suggests that the objection is motivated by instrumentalist convictions: reasoning leading to action on the basis of alleged practical inductions is reduced to theoretical inductions together with instrumental reasoning. (In our example, general facts about hot polenta, inductively arrived at, together with means-end reasoning proceeding from those facts, and from desires bearing on them, to a desire to eat hot polenta.) If that is right, the objection should not seem pressing at this point in the argument. We have just established in Chapter 2 that instrumental reasoning cannot stand on its own, and we are now investigating practical induction as a means of filling the ensuing gap. If this method of eliminating practical induction could be applied across the board, it would put us back to square one: instrumental reasoning would again be the only form of practical reasoning, and all practical reasoning would have to bottom out in desires one just has. But if our arguments have been successful, that cannot be what we are after. While *some* practical inductions may be reducible in this way, this is not the time to insist that they must *all* be. I am going to proceed on the assumption that instrumentalism is out of the way, and if it is, then the reductionist objection is unmotivated.[5]

§ 3.2

How can we show that practical induction is a pattern of practical inference? Or, what comes to the same thing, given that inference is first and foremost a normative notion, how can we show that practical induction is a legitimate method to use in thinking one's way through

---

5. If it were to turn out that practical induction was the *only* possible alternative to means-end reasoning, then invoking the conclusions of Chapter 2 would be not just a way of showing the proposed across-the-board elimination of practical induction to be unmotivated: it would be a *reductio ad absurdum* of the proposal.

practical problems? One way that philosophers have tackled the problem of induction—that is, the traditional problem of showing that theoretical induction, the induction of general facts from particular facts, is a legitimate form of inference—is to try to show that induction is guaranteed to work: that if, for example, you observe a number of black ravens, and, following the rules of inductive inference, conclude that all ravens are black, you can be sure that you will never come across ravens of any other color. (A slightly more sophisticated version of this approach would try to show that you will *probably* never come across ravens of any other color.) That is, they treat the problem of induction as though what were missing, and what they were trying to provide, were reassurances like those supplied by an assembly line's quality control unit.

I'm not going to try to show that practical induction is legitimate by showing that when you use it, it is guaranteed to work. My reason, once again, is that I am using philosophical experience with theoretical induction as a guide in approaching its practical analog: a good deal of effort has been squandered on this approach without making much headway on solving the traditional problem of induction in its terms. This suggests taking some other approach to practical induction.

Not all attempted inductions are equally likely to succeed. For example, inductions that deploy the predicate 'is a raven' are much more likely to result in successful inferences about the colors of avian plumage than those that use the predicate 'is a raven that I've seen or a robin that I haven't'. A relative or variant of the problem of induction, sometimes called the 'new riddle' of induction, is roughly the problem of separating those inductions that are reasonable and likely to work from those which aren't and won't.[6] The approach that calls for a warranty is likely to call as well for operating instructions telling the customer what problems the inferential device ought to be applied to. But for the same reasons that I won't try to supply a warranty, I won't try to provide operating instructions, either: the new riddle is another of those philosophical problems that have acquired an air of intractability, which I will take to be a reason for circumnavigating its practical analog. So in arguing that practical

---

6. Goodman, 1979. See Stalker, 1994, for a recent survey of the literature.

induction is legitimate, I'm not going to try to provide a way of saying *which* practical inductions are likely to work.

If I am not going to supply a warranty, or the accompanying operating instructions, in just what sense do I propose to establish the legitimacy of practical induction? I will try to show that, in the course of practical deliberation, one must treat practical induction as effective, whether or not one has a guarantee that it is; and that this requirement suffices to legitimize practical induction. Let me explain. When one engages in practical deliberation, one is trying, directly or indirectly, to address the practical question, "What should I do?" (I'm going to leave to one side cases where one deliberates on another's behalf, as when one means to give advice, and cases in which one deliberates as part of a group.) Now in the course of trying to answer this question, one may suppose that there is an *I* that could act on an answer to it. After all, if there were not, the question would have no practical point.[7] The supposition is legitimate not because it is known to be true—if it were known to be true it would not have to be *supposed*—but because it needs to be, as it were, taken for granted for the sake of the argument. When one is engaging in practical deliberation, the assumption that one is an acting self is authorized by its dialectical context.

A good deal is required in order for one to be the kind of acting self for which practical deliberation makes sense. For instance, if there is nothing one is *able* to do, there is not much point in thinking about what one *should* do: agency involves the availability of resources, options, and, in one way or another, power.[8] I'm not going to try to spell out everything that is needed if one is to be a full-fledged agent; instead,

---

7. To be sure, one can plan for eventualities in which one will not be present, as when one makes out a will, or buys life insurance. However, one cannot plan what one will *do* in such eventualities; rather, one plans to take action when one can in hopes of having effects on those later times when one will not be able to intervene oneself. A very similar point holds for cases in which one plans for periods of impaired agency, as when Ulysses had himself tied to the mast. I will consider a related skeptical worry below.

8. Much of what at first glance might seem to be practical deliberation in the absence of options is actually daydreaming, as when one whiles away the afternoon considering what one would do if one had a million dollars. (I'm grateful to Julia Driver for the example.)

I will focus on an aspect of agency that is somewhat closer to home than the means one has for working one's will in the world. In the course of practical deliberation, one can take it that one is a *unified* agent— or rather, bearing in mind that unified agency is a matter of degree, that one is unified enough for one's practical deliberations to have a point. (I will say a bit more about what I mean by this in a moment.) And by the same reasoning, one can take it, for purposes of practical deliberation, that anything that must be the case in order for one to be a unified agent, *is* the case. So I'm going to argue that practical induction is legitimate in the following sense: its effectiveness is a precondition for unity of agency, from which it follows that, *within* the context of practical deliberation, it can be treated as a legitimate form of inference. That is, when you are trying to answer a practical question, you are within your rights using practical induction to do so.

The argument will hit the beach in three waves. First, in this chapter, I will trace out a picture of unity of agency. Unity of agency, I will claim, consists in our ability to square our conflicting concerns, interests, and priorities, and the way we do this turns out to depend on bridging or connecting judgments that, as a matter of fact, we obtain through practical induction. This chapter and the next fill in the picture of unity of agency from the inside out—that is, by considering what intelligent choice looks like to the person making it. As I fill in the picture, I will be introducing a fair number of what, during this stretch of the argument, I am going to treat as brute facts. Not all of these will be uncontroversial. For example, I will claim that all, or just about all, practical inference is defeasible; this may well raise the hackles of readers brought up in philosophical traditions that see morality as derived, top-down, from a single and exceptionless principle.

In the next chapter, I will argue that this dependence on practical induction is not optional: there is no other source for the requisite mediating judgments that will do the job of unifying agency. I will explain what any workable alternative to practical induction would have to do, describe a dummy alternative that would work if anything could, and show that it could not possibly do the job. Once again, the argument will invoke facts about human agency that I will treat as brute, but which I expect to be recognizable in anyone's experience of practical deliberation:

most notably, that one can discover that there are things one just cannot put up with.

Finally, in Chapter 5, I will turn to explaining *why* we have no alternative to practical induction, and to showing how the facts about human agency used in the argument up to that point are not simply brute, after all. To do this, I will shift perspective, and develop the picture of agency from the outside in—that is, from the point of view of a designer trying to construct an agent able to cope with the kinds of environments human beings have to face. Once an unavoidable feature of those environments is identified, the various pieces of the puzzle I have left up in the air will fall into place: to anticipate, it is only by learning from experience that we can successfully field the surprises that are bound to come our way.

§ 3.3

Unity of agency is the practical aspect of a more general phenomenon, that of unity of the self. Now a useful rule of thumb in thinking about unity of the self at a time, as contrasted with unity of the self over time, or about synchronic as opposed to diachronic personal identity, might be this: if two thoughts belong to the same mind, then there is a train of thought available to that mind in which they could both figure. If there were some mental item, allegedly mine, that I could not use in any of my cogitations whatsoever, it would be hard to see what the point of insisting that it was mine could be; indeed, it is hard to see how I could so much as notice its existence. And conversely, if there were some thought that regularly played a part in my thinking, it would be hard to imagine better evidence for its being *my* thought.[9]

Of course, unity of the self is a matter of degree; so we can say that a mind is (synchronically) unified to the extent that when one thought or mental item becomes relevant to a train of thought that does not yet include it, it is likely to be successfully brought to bear on that train

---

9. Trains of thought usually take time, which suggests that attempts to prise apart synchronic and diachronic unity of agency may be ultimately unsuccessful. The distinction is heuristically valuable nonetheless.

of thought. If hearing so-and-so's voice would remind me of a recent dream in which he figured, that goes some distance toward showing that the aural experience and the dream belong to the same mind. But only *some* distance: a would-be mind held together by associative connections alone would be little more than a Humean bundle of mental contents, which is to say, not a unified mind at all. More important is the ability of a thought to figure in inferences: if hearing him makes me revise my assumption that he has not come in today, that is, if my assumption and my experience-derived belief are conjoined as premises of a bit of reasoning, that contributes more significantly towards there being a single owner of both the belief and the assumption. Conversely, if my prejudices about his work habits are inferentially insulated from my observations of his work habits, then my mind is less unified than it might be. There are inferences in which one's thought could appropriately figure; the more of these it is prone to figure in, the more fully the thought is part of one's mind—and, by the same token, the more unified one's mind is. (Let me say straight out that this is not intended as a definition or analysis or specification of necessary and sufficient conditions for unity of the self at a time. While I am trying to say what unity of the self consists in, I am not trying to give a definition of what it is for a collection of mental states to add up to a mind, or even a definition of what it is to own a mental state.)

No human mind is fully unified; there are perhaps reasons to think that nothing complex enough to be a mind could be.[10] Our personalities are more integrated in some ways than others. The absent-minded professor may have his specialization at his fingertips, even though he cannot collect his wits about him when almost any other subject is on the table; and his training in critically assessing arguments may be left far behind as soon as, say, political topics are broached. Someone may have a perspicuous view of the ways in which he is allowing his life to slide out of control; that is, the side of him that does theoretical reasoning may be more unified than the side that reasons practically. I said a moment ago that unity of the self is a matter of degree, but we can now see that this

---

10. Cherniak, 1986, pp. 128f, sketches an argument that I expect could be adapted to support this hypothesis.

turn of phrase may be misleading: a mind can be more cohesive in some areas than others; and lack of cohesion can manifest itself in many qualitatively different ways. All this is concealed by quantitative locutions like 'degree' and 'extent', with their suggestion of a simple scale capable of summing up the detailed and idiosyncratic ways in which minds may be, or fail to be, unified. I will use these locutions anyway; avoiding them quickly becomes too tedious and longwinded to be justifiable. But we should not forget what they are a shorthand for. The long and short of it is that, although no mind is fully unified, those of us who are more or less getting by are unified enough to—more or less—get by.

Unity of the self in the practical domain will in like manner be exhibited in one's ability to—and in the likelihood that one actually *will*—bring to bear, in the course of practical deliberation, one's practical judgments (and, of course, other items in one's mental inventory) as they become relevant to the question one is considering. At one extreme, someone in whom action is triggered by whatever impulse happens to come over him, without any regard to other concerns or interests he may have, is a mere collection of reflexes rather than a cohesive acting self. At the other, the thoughtful deliberator whose every decision is appropriately informed by the full range of considerations available to him is the *phronimos,* Aristotle's unattainable ideal of practical intelligence, unified agency, and virtue.

Between the extremes of infancy and wisdom lies the modicum of coherence that we demand of responsible adults, and it is in this region that I want to take a look at some of the ways in which two aspects of unity of agency are connected. We have been considering an internal hallmark of practical unity: the ability to bring one's practical judgments to bear when they become relevant to one's practical deliberations—which is not to be sharply distinguished from the tendency to exercise that ability. But agency is often seen from the outside; and from the external standpoint, unity of agency appears as coherence in an agent's plans and activities. This external coherence is not merely consistency of character, the brute tendency to do the same kind of thing in similar situations. Someone may waffle and hedge frequently enough for others to regard his indecisiveness as (they say) just like him; but his behavior seen from the middle distance makes him out to be scattered and unfocused. The practically

unified agent coordinates his actions so that they reflect a set of sufficiently organized priorities. When unity of agency frays at the edges, we
encounter vacillation, weakness of will (or akrasia), self-deception, areas
of compulsive or merely habitual action, and other related phenomena.

The internal and external hallmarks of unity (and disunity) of agency
are closely linked. Suppose that I have available two practical judgments
capable of serving as the major premises of practical syllogisms—say, that
it is important to help the down and out, and that I need to maintain
a fairly tight rein on my budget. If I am reasonably good at bringing
to bear my practical judgments when they become relevant, then, when
a panhandler sets going a practical syllogism proceeding from the first
premise ('It's important to help the down-and-out; this guy's down and
out; let me help him'), I remember that I cannot afford to be extravagant,
and I fork over the single rather than the five. And when I'm making
up my budget ('I need to make cuts; charity is somewhere I could cut;
let's cut charitable contributions'), if I recall the importance of helping
the down-and-out I will not simply delete charity from my list. The
upshot is plans and actions that cohere with one another and appear to
be modulated by a serviceable picture of what matters. In other words,
the internal aspect of unity of agency tends to produce, and so explains,
the presence of the external aspect.

Suppose, however, that when I consider what to do on the basis of
one practical judgment, other relevant practical judgments do not get
successfully brought to bear. In order to bring my spending under control, I resolve to cease contributing to charity; but faced with a panhandler, I reach into my pocket and come up with a twenty. My behavior
is likely to seem weak-willed, or self-deceptive, or vacillating, or even, in
extreme cases, reminiscent of a split personality (these types of behavior
are not always, even in principle, distinguishable); and I'm likely to find
myself regretting my actions fairly frequently. That is, when internally
characterized unity of agency is on the wane, externally characterized
unity of agency will normally start to lapse as well.

We can tie the various loose strands together by returning to the practical syllogism. Practical syllogisms are—by contrast with reflexes, or,
what amounts to the same thing, exceptionless rules—*defeasible*. This
means that practical syllogisms are sensitive to the presence of defeating

conditions. My inference from 'The car gets washed on Mondays' and 'Today is Monday' to 'Time to wash the car', although normally perfectly in order, is defeated when it turns out that Margie must be driven to the emergency room.[11] Because not all defeating conditions can be anticipated ahead of time, any exceptionless rule, no matter how complicated, can be conjoined with circumstances that make its application look mindless: if I go ahead and wash the car while Margie bleeds to death, I will be displaying compulsive behavior—or perhaps others will see at work an animosity toward Margie of which I am not myself aware. An intelligent sensitivity to the defeasibility conditions of one's practical syllogisms is part of what makes one a practical reasoner rather than a reflex-driven robot; sensitivity of this kind is a matter of degree, and is an index of practical unity of the self.[12] For unity of agency is a matter of bringing to bear one's practical judgments when they become relevant to deliberation; but this is precisely to deploy defeasible practical syllogisms, rather than to be subject to the exceptionless reflexes they become as this sensitivity is lost. An agent is synchronically unified to the degree that his practical syllogisms are defeasible.[13]

---

11. Defeasible inferences are sometimes contrasted with deductive inferences: you can be sure, of a deductively valid inference from true premises, that its conclusion is true, and that you will not have to retract it no matter what further information you subsequently run across, provided that information does not impugn either the soundness or the validity of the inference. The distinction made in the AI lexicon, between monotonic and non-monotonic reasoning, also captures more or less this contrast.

12. I don't mean to be unfair to the robots. If we allow that robots could be built to exhibit this kind of sensitivity, then a variant of my argument will purport to show that they too would have to learn their goals from experience. To the best of my knowledge, this is an issue that has received almost no attention from the engineering community.

13. But can't unity of agency be a matter of what gets called 'having principles'—that is, principles one is unwilling to compromise under *any* circumstances? To be sure, one might have principles that never do get overridden, because no situation arises in which they should be. And this need not impugn unity of agency; the sensitivity to competing concerns involved in defeasibility may be there even if the principle is never in fact defeated. But if the rule is never overridden because the requisite sensitivity is not there, we have, not flinty integrity, but pigheadedness.

It's worth mentioning a class of apparent exceptions, those in which the defeasibility is legislated into the antecedent of the rule rather than being left to its application. 'Do not murder' (by contrast with 'Do not kill') seems as inexorable as it does because we

I stated earlier that one is permitted in the course of practical deliberation to assume that one is a (sufficiently) unified agent, and consequently, to assume that the preconditions of unified agency are satisfied. We have now seen that one is a synchronically unified agent to the extent that one's practical syllogisms are defeasible. So one may in the course of practical deliberation suppose that one's practical syllogisms are defeasible (enough). We now need to take a closer look at what defeasibility involves.

§ 3.4

Defeasibility in one's practical syllogisms requires bringing to bear competing considerations when they become salient. Now there is more to bringing a competing consideration to bear than simply recalling it: the weak-willed dieter may guiltily remember that his diet does not allow him another helping of cheesecake, but he still goes ahead and finishes off a second plateful. (As Aristotle remarked, in cases like these the competing consideration is not so much figuring into the train of reasoning as being recited, in something like the way an actor recites his lines.)[14] But it might be thought that what is missing here is the routine functioning of some rather simple, indeed semiautomatic, mental machinery. The dieter's mental kitchen scale may be temporarily disabled, but when the machinery is in order, nothing more is needed for integrating the potentially defeating condition into one's would-be practical syllogism than realizing that, in the circumstances at hand, the two considerations are relevant to each other. On this view, one of the two salient considerations is more important than the other: one weighs the competing considerations, and acts on the basis of the strongest—or, where several factors are in play, on the basis of the set of jointly compatible considerations with the greatest summed strength or weight.

---

treat many defeating conditions (self-defense, one's duty as a soldier or policeman or executioner, the request of the dying man in agony, and so on) as reasons to withhold the description 'murder'. The defeasibility remains in substance even as it is concealed by the treatment of the terminology. (For pressing me on these points, I'm grateful to Sarah Buss, Julia Driver, and Wilfried Hinsch.)

14. *NE* 1147a15–25.

There are, of course, cases in which one can produce quantitative comparisons of this kind. But the idea that one can always do so, or that one can do so most of the time, is a relic of the instrumentalist model of practical reasoning. On that model, the brute having of desires justifies action that satisfies them; and, on a very common variant of the model, desires have strengths that allow any two desires (or groups of desires) to be compared and prioritized: one desire's being stronger than another justifies satisfying the former rather than the latter. But the resulting picture of deliberation as the arranging of the respective desires on one's mental scale turns out to be mistaken for the same reasons that instrumentalism more generally is mistaken.

In the last chapter we saw that the forward-directed inferential commitments involved in a desire must be matched by suitable backward-directed commitments. (In plainer, though slightly imprecise, English, a desire's origins must, in one's own view, underwrite the inferences one regards as ensuing from it.) The strength of a desire is just a pattern of forward-directed inferential commitments: the strengths of desires encode information about how desires ought to fare in comparisons with each other.[15] Now on the way of thinking that takes reasoning with a desire (or other practical judgment) to consist in the routine comparative assessment of already-available strengths or weights, those strengths must encode the upshots of all possible practical comparisons the agent might make. But when we think about what the backward-directed commitments corresponding to the strength of a desire must look like, we will see that deciding which of two considerations is more important by comparing their strengths must be the exception rather than the rule.

When one forms a desire, or arrives at a practical judgment, the deliberations on the basis of which one does so are inevitably quite restricted in scope. When I decide I want to travel to Prague, I do so in the context of considering a very limited number of alternatives—say, Moscow, Leipzig, and perhaps Budapest. I cannot stop to consider *all* the alternatives, if I am ever to get around to traveling at all. This means that if my

---

15. Because strengths are also seen as quantities, there are constraints on which patterns of comparisons can be so encoded; but this family of issues won't concern us here.

newly-formed desire is not to involve me in backward-directed commitments I cannot meet, then although I may be in a position to report that my desire to visit Prague is stronger than my desire to visit Moscow, my desire will prove to have no definite relative strength with respect to such other options as travel to Tokyo, or becoming a monk, or taking voice lessons, and so on.

Of course, my judgment can be informed by and import other considerations already at hand; these may be considerations of greater generality. A year in Thailand, for example, is simply out of the question because I have already determined that travel must not interfere with work. But the more general considerations can themselves only have been formed on the basis of quite limited deliberation. And so they themselves cannot normally contribute the content that would be required for the strengths instrumentalists suppose desires to have.

Our desires do not normally have the strengths that would support comparisons with arbitrary other desires, and now it is clear why. The point of a desire is to guide action. A desire whose content far outruns the thought that one could have put into it is bound to get one into trouble when it is put to use; because one will find oneself committed to courses of action that one has not seriously considered, it will be a poor guide. The vast majority of possible comparisons between desires had better not have their outcomes already encoded into those desires' strengths; someone who did form desires whose strengths permitted comparisons with arbitrary other desires would be making a serious practical blunder.

The forward-directed inferential commitments involved in the kind of strengths of desire that would permit arbitrary comparisons between desires require backward-directed inferential commitments that could not possibly be met. So it is not surprising that strengths of desires are in fact rather sketchy, and that when novel comparisons between competing judgments are at hand, they do not play much of a role. The upshot for our present purposes is that the defeasibility conditions of practical syllogisms are not simply a matter of the respective strengths of a syllogism's major premise and of the potentially defeating consideration. Bringing a practical judgment to bear in the course of one's practical reasoning is, most of the time, more than just remembering it and allowing it to weigh in.

§ 3.5

If not by some semi-automatic procedure of weighing one consideration against another, how does one determine whether a potentially defeating consideration ought to abort the progress of a practical syllogism one has underway? Consider the following example:[16]

Alison works for Devil's Island Repertory Theatre, but she is negotiating the terms of a new and more interesting job at the Tragic Mews, down the coast. She does not yet have a contract in hand, and she has a policy of not giving notice, or letting it be known that she is planning to leave a job, until the next job is settled: she does not want to fall between two chairs, or have undercut her effectiveness if she ends up staying.

Tomorrow the Devil's Island management will make plans for the coming season. Alison will be at the meeting, and sticking by her policy will mean lying; her lies will become the basis of her colleagues' almost-sure-to-be-disrupted plans. Alison is averse to lying, because she feels loyal to her colleagues and the organization of which they are a part. Which of the two competing practical judgments should take precedence in these circumstances? Is the practical syllogism that tells her to keep her plans to herself defeasible by her aversion to lying?

Alison cannot say which of the two considerations she feels more strongly, which is not to say that she is indifferent; her desires do not have strengths that can decide the practical problem for her. But she realizes that were her current employers planning to fire her, they would not tell her, if there were business reasons not to. And she thinks that it is generally inappropriate to show more loyalty to others than they are prepared to show to oneself. (Certainly, she muses, one would be a fool to feel guiltier about it than *they* would.) She decides to continue to play her cards close to her chest; until she has a signed contract in hand, she will act as though she is staying on at her current job.

---

16. I'm grateful to Meg Patterson for the example. I should perhaps add that the deliberations described here are not her own.

Before moving on to the next example, let me highlight a few features of this one. First, the way in which the practical problem is solved is ad hoc. I believe that this is typical: there is no semi-automatic procedure that can be successfully applied regardless of the specifics of the conflicting judgments. Alison looks around for resources that she can use to solve the problem, and she is fortunate in having at hand a consideration that restricts the scope of one of the competing practical judgments in a way that cleanly effects a solution. (Other considerations that Alison surveyed—for example, that keeping secrets is stressful, that lying is generally a bad thing, and that lying would be bound to affect her professional reputation adversely—did not do the job. It is also worth noticing the role of straightforwardly factual considerations; had she believed her current employers would have given her advance notice of impending dismissal, this resolution of the problem would not have been available.) There is no guarantee that such considerations will always be there when they are needed.

Second, and again I think this is typical, solving the problem involved bringing to bear a further practical judgment: that one should not be more loyal to others than they are prepared to be toward oneself. This practical judgment is not introduced as merely another competing desire or concern; it does not weigh in against the other judgments it is being conjoined with. (The original problem was to adjudicate between two competing general practical judgments; just adding another would transform this into the more complicated problem of adjudicating between three competing general practical judgments.) Rather, it *connects* the two considerations already at work. The major premises of the two competing practical syllogisms have their respective points.[17] The point of not lying to one's coworkers has to do with one's loyalty to and professional respect for them. And the point of playing one's cards close to one's chest is a matter of the responsibility one must take for one's own interests and life. Loyalty, when it is more than dog-like attachment to a master, involves restraint and limits; the relevant limits are suggested by Alison's concern for her interests, which draws her attention to her em-

---

17. Cf. Chapter 2, note 17. These are not always further goals, although in particular cases they might be.

ployers' very similar responsibility for their own interests.[18] A reasonable loyalty does not demand action that would not—and on her understanding of her employers' responsibilities, should not—be reciprocated.

Third, the connecting practical judgment is neither a particular judgment, nor one of the extremely general variety of practical judgments popular among moral philosophers. A particular judgment—one amounting to the decision that *now* one had better do *this*—would bypass deliberation in favor of somehow just knowing what to do. But one engages in practical deliberation when one does *not* know what to do, that is, when particular judgments of this kind are not to be had. And experiment shows that extremely general practical judgments—such as Kant's Categorical Imperative, to the effect that one should always do what one could will to be a universal law, or the dictum that one ought always to do what will make one happy—turn out to play very little role in adjudicating conflicts between practical judgments of lower generality.[19] Plausible practical judgments of a very high level of generality tend to be insufficiently substantive, to lack the nitty-gritty needed for solving problems like Alison's. The practical judgments that are neither particular nor extremely general, or practical judgments of an intermediate level of generality, I will call *somewhat general* practical judgments.

Finally, we can say something about how Alison came to have the problem-resolving practical judgment at hand. Over the course of her

---

18. The failure of loyalty as an unrestricted guiding virtue is compellingly portrayed in Ishiguro, 1989. Of course, what matters now is not whether this view of loyalty is correct, but whether Alison thinks it is.

19. This should not be too surprising. As to the first, Kant himself seems to have thought that perfect duties could not conflict, so that the Categorical Imperative does not need to adjudicate between them. (Kant's discussion of perfect duties, and most famously of lying, shows that he failed to see how central a characteristic of practical reasoning defeasibility actually is.) And he took conflicts between imperfect duties to be resolved by judgment—read, the particular practical judgments discussed a moment ago—and casuistry, which is most charitably construed as the process we are now considering.

Kant is also the locus classicus for the explanation of the fact that appeals to happiness are not particularly useful in guiding particular choices. It is a deep fact about us, Kant argued, that we are not able to know enough about what happiness is to make use of it in that way (1785/1981, Ak. 418).

life, Alison has had both first-person experience, and first-hand observation, of unreciprocated loyalty. In just about every case, she has found
that it works out badly: one is exploited, betrayed, walked all over; or one
ends up putting off one's partner; or one just feels that one has lost one's
self-respect and sold oneself short. Generalizing from these instances, Alison has concluded that there needs to be balance and proportion in
loyalty and commitment. That is, the connecting practical judgment is
the conclusion of a practical induction.

Here is a second, rather different example:

> Beth is a philosopher who has adopted a policy of not going to talks by
> visiting speakers; they do not, she has found, contain the advertised new
> insights, incisive arguments, or horizon-broadening ideas, but rather, by
> and large, just the same old moves in a slightly different order from last
> time. This week a visitor is coming with whom Beth would like to go to
> dinner after the talk; she feels it would be embarrassing to turn up for
> the food after having skipped the paper. Should she make an exception
> to her policy?
>
> Beth realizes that if she is bored by the talk, she will find dinner
> unenjoyable. For one thing, if the talk turns out to have been typically
> boring, she will have stopped paying attention midway through, and will
> be just as embarrassed by not knowing what went on as she would have
> been by not having come at all. For another, if the talk is as bad as the
> statistics indicate it will be, a philosophical conversation with the speaker
> is likely to be undesirable. For the same reasons one should not bother
> to go to hear speakers, one should not, Beth decides, have dinner with
> them afterward.
>
> However, the reason that Beth wants to have dinner with this speaker
> is that she has read the speaker's work, and it is usually exciting, full
> of new insights, fresh arguments, and so on. There is every reason to
> expect that his work-in-progress will be just as good. And this makes
> it likely that his talk will be an exception to the practical judgment
> that philosophy talks are not worth going to. Beth decides to make an
> exception, just this once.

This case is very different from the previous one, but the remarks
made earlier apply to it as well. Like its predecessor, the solution to

the problem is improvised from materials at hand. Appeal is made to the points of the major premises of the competing practical syllogisms. (Speakers are not worth hearing because they tend to be competently professional rather than deep or even clever; one dines with speakers because one expects philosophically exciting table conversation.) A somewhat general practical judgment—that this speaker's work is for the most part philosophically exciting—is used to connect the competing practical judgments; this connecting practical judgment is itself the product of a practical induction.

It is worth remarking that, in both examples, the connecting practical judgment is not the only one that is likely to be produced by practical induction. Beth's view that speakers are not worth hearing was the upshot of what must have seemed like interminable experience. And although it is not part of the story, Alison's policy of not letting on that one plans to leave might well have been arrived at through practical induction as well. We will see why this is important in the next chapter.

§ 3.6

I claimed earlier that agents are unified roughly to the extent that their practical syllogisms are defeasible. The pair of examples we have looked at suggest that bringing a potentially defeating consideration to bear on a practical syllogism often involves further practical judgments; these enable the gears of the competing interests to engage one another. I do not want to claim that conflicts between practical judgments must always be resolved by using further connecting judgments of this kind; such a claim would be hard to square with my view that defeasibility in one's practical syllogisms requires inventiveness, improvisation, and an ability to fly by the seat of one's pants. And we have in any case seen only a couple of examples.[20] While I cannot here demonstrate by enumeration how common this use of inductively derived practical judgments is, I think that surveying a number of such problems and their solutions—and at this point the reader is invited to undertake such a

---

20. For a couple more, see Millgram, 1997a. In section 5.4 we will see why such connecting judgments so often play a large role in adjudicating conflicts.

survey himself—will show that much of the time such connecting judgments are essential, and prove to have been inductively arrived at.

Within the context of solving a practical problem, one may proceed
on the assumption that one is a unified agent. Unity of agency requires
that one have available an adequate supply of the kind of practical judgments used in rendering one's practical syllogisms defeasible inferences;
it follows that one may suppose, when practical deliberation is underway,
that one's stock is, or can be made, adequate. That recapitulation of our
location in the argument can be made more concrete. The argument can
be directed to both the synchronic and diachronic dimensions of unity
of agency, and because it will turn out to be important later on, I will
run through each.

Suppose I were so absent-minded that whenever I considered what
to do, I overlooked or otherwise failed properly to take into account
the most important relevant considerations. If I were as scatterbrained as
that, the outcomes of my deliberations would almost always be mistaken,
and would normally not be worth acting on. And that means that if my
present practical deliberations are to have a point, I must be the kind
of being that usually does at least an adequate job of taking relevant
considerations into account. But to be such a being is, I have argued,
to be a synchronically unified agent. So I must suppose, when I am
deliberating, that I am now a synchronically unified agent.

A less abbreviated form of the argument exploits both the fact that
effective agency must be temporally extended and that it must be synchronically unified. For practical deliberation to have a point, there must
be someone (oneself, in the first-person singular case we are considering)
on the receiving end who can be expected to act on the conclusion of
one's deliberations. The conclusion of one's deliberations may be a single
practical judgment to be executed immediately, but more typically it is
a complex of particular and general practical judgments amounting (depending on its overall level of generality) to a plan or to a policy. Plans
take time to carry out, and policies take even longer; this is partly because the conditions they are responding to occur over time, and partly
because people can only do one thing, or at most a very few things, at a
time. And this means that before the time comes to execute my plan, or
while I am in the middle of it, new issues and concerns may arise that

will be, or that will seem to me to be, relevant to whether I ought to go through with it. In fact, if the plan is at all interesting, they are bound to arise; any plan or policy ambitious enough to be significant entails some sacrifice or other, and the impending sacrifice will naturally (even if only akratically) raise the question: is it worth it?

Now if I am counting on being able to execute the plan or policy about which I am deliberating, I need to be able to assume that it (probably) won't be bumped aside, for no good reason, by the first whim to come along—that I won't be weak-willed about my plan, or vacillating and dithering about whether to go through with it, and so on. The plan or policy must be *stable*.[21] Because competing considerations, whimsical and otherwise, inevitably *do* come along, that means supposing that I will dismiss them when they are not good reasons to abandon the policy; and this means being able to bring the considerations supporting my plan to bear on the practical inferences triggered by its competitors, in ways like those we have been examining.

Then again, one does not wish the conclusion of one's deliberation to be executed blindly, come what may. Because plans and policies take time to carry out, almost none of them will succeed, or even make sense, without adjustments along the way to accommodate issues and problems and new information that come up. Of the clumsy, inflexible and robotic execution of plans, we can say: there is no point in deliberating if one's plans are going to be executed like *that*.[22] But the alternative to such stultifying inflexibility requires considering reasons to change or abandon

---

21. For a recent discussion of related issues, see Bratman, 1992.

22. The story of Sphex, now part of philosophers' lore, is both a familiar illustration of this point and an occasion for addressing an objection that has been pending for a few pages. (See Dennett, 1984; his account comes from Wolldridge, 1963, p. 82.) Sphex is a wasp whose agency is so minimal as to seem a likely counterexample to my claim that unified agency requires defeasibility: although its rules are not defeasible, it has so few of them that they cannot conflict, and the actions that result from following them add up to a coherent plan for providing its young a place to hatch and a well-stocked larder.

But—the well-known story goes—humans can intervene to trigger Sphex's rules in ways that produce pointless, repetitive behavior. When defeasibility is lacking, it is always possible to find circumstances in which the agent's internal lack of connectedness—concealed before in the fortunate fit between circumstances and policy—comes to the fore in a medley of senseless actions. Even when a reflex-driven agent is, like Sphex,

one's plan as they come up, and making intelligent decisions that factor in those reasons. Again, this means bringing to bear potentially defeating considerations in ways like those we have described.

For first-person practical deliberation to have a point, the deliberating agent must be presumed to be around in the future in which the plans and policies that are deliberatively arrived at are to be implemented; and the agent at that future time must be synchronically unified if those plans and policies are to be successfully carried out. So I may (while I am deliberating) suppose that I am a temporally extended agent whose future self is synchronically unified. In other words, if one supposes there is a point to deliberating, one is committed to supposing that one will, by and large, be able to handle candidate reasons to abandon or adjust one's conclusion, as they come up. But if being able to do this requires having an adequate stock of practical judgments that can be used for this purpose—practical judgments that are somewhat general, relevant to the domain in which one is reasoning, and so on—supposing that one will be able to handle candidate reasons involves supposing that one's stock *is* (or will be) adequate.

As it happens, experience reassures us that our stock of somewhat general practical judgments is, for enough of the contingencies in which we find ourselves, more or less adequate; it also tells us that an indispensable portion, perhaps an absolute preponderance, of these are arrived at via practical induction. We have not yet seen why practical induction *has* to be a primary supplier of these judgments; I have, so far, only claimed that, if we look, we will find that it is. In the next chapter, I will argue that practical induction is in fact a necessary source of these judgments; once we take this further step, we will have shown that we are committed to, and licensed in, supposing that practical induction works.

---

trivially unified, in the face of this kind of manipulation, it will fail to project unified agency into its world.

4

Doing without Learning

Experience, I have suggested, shows that practical induction is responsible for much of such unity of agency as we manage to achieve. The reach of this point, however, falls short of a satisfactory justification of the inference pattern. As creatures who rely on the results of practical induction in the cognitive exercises through which we attain unity of agency, we are committed to practical induction's reasonableness and efficacy, in something like the way that drivers are committed to the effectiveness of automobiles as a means of transportation. But to acknowledge this is not yet to have shown that our use of practical induction is a matter of necessity (the kind of necessity that is the mother of invention); for perhaps there is an alternative source of the practical judgments we need for unity of agency, and perhaps, even if we are, now, dependent on practical induction, this means only that we should be weaning ourselves away from it. That one has become accustomed to driving does not show that one should not give it up and start taking the train.

To show that unity of agency presupposes the usability of practical induction, we need to show that alternatives to practical induction are not available. Again, we are not trying to provide a manufacturer's warranty for practical induction, but to show that it is legitimate by showing that, whether or not it is guaranteed to work, we have no choice but to act, and to reason about acting, on the assumption that it does. Showing that we have no choice requires showing that we have no *other* choice, and we need to consider first what kind of argument might establish that conclusion.

§ 4.1

There are a number of apparent alternatives to practical induction already on the philosophical menu. One might try to derive one's decisions from one, or a few, very general principles: hedonism, understood as the idea that one ought to perform the action that gives oneself, or others, the most pleasure, might be an example of such a principle. Then there are the layers of instinct, habit, prejudice, inclination, and personal quirkiness that a Kantian might call empirical character, and which might serve as a guide when considerations conflict. Or a policy of adjusting one's system of ends in the direction of greater coherence might seem promising: what effect such a policy will have is going to depend, in part, on just what coherence is taken to be; but, given the understanding of unity of agency with which we are working, it seems likely that on most plausible renditions of coherence, the more coherence, the more unity. Kant's Categorical Imperative can be read as a relative of this last proposal, in that it imposes a complicated consistency condition on one's intentions, part of which is the requirement that like cases be treated alike. Consistency of this kind is, again, a plausible contributor to unity of agency. More arbitrarily, one might simply adopt some entirely exceptionless rule, for instance, the precept of that character of Saki's who "in his wildest lapses into veracity never admits to being more than twenty-two."[1]

There is obviously no point in trying to show that we need practical induction by disposing of the alternatives one by one. The menu I have started to present is necessarily incomplete, since, with a little imagination, such possibilities can be multiplied indefinitely. An argument with a conclusion of the requisite generality must proceed by identifying constraints on viable alternatives to practical induction, with the object of

---

1. Compare Watterson, 1993, p. 79.

showing that nothing could satisfy them all. I will elicit three such necessary conditions, and use them to describe a representative stand-in for the range of alternatives to practical induction. I will then navigate the representative alternative through the map of the problem it faces. Each of the streets, we will see, terminates in a dead end.

We can get the first of these constraints onto the board by considering empirical character, which is probably the most down-to-earth entry on the scattershot menu of alternatives we just glanced over. Empirical character will not do in that it is too systematically contaminated by the conclusions of practical induction to serve as an alternative to it. One's character is made up in large part of the results, worn down or blurred in transmission, or haphazardly accreted, of past practical inductions, performed by oneself or by others; if one were somehow to subtract the influence of practical induction from an individual's character, one would be left with very little. (Even biological instincts are often generated by processes that mimic practical induction.) Empirical character looks like a promising alternative because it is often not foolish to rely on it. But the reason its deliverances are frequently sensible is that there are practical inductions in its background—and so the very source of its appeal is also why it cannot, at this point in the argument, be appealed to: the constraint in play, which we can now make explicit, on what an alternative to practical induction can look like is that an *alternative* to practical induction must not help itself, directly or indirectly, to the results of practical induction.

It's important to see that relying on empirical character indirectly produced by the practical inductions of others is, for present purposes, on a par with relying on practical inductions of one's own. We are trying to show that agents must think of practical induction as an inferential pattern legitimately available to them within their own practical deliberations. Accepting as bases for inference the deliverances of others' practical inductions is, as we saw in Chapter 2, to accept the legitimacy of the method that produced them; one cannot then go on to insist that *further* applications of the method, by others or by oneself, would be illegitimate. If someone accepts the assertions made by his physics textbook because they were arrived at through the scientific method, he must think that the scientific method would be a legitimate technique for him to apply too. (One can be committed to the legitimacy of the scientific method even if one has never practiced it oneself.)

Practical induction is our label for the way in which we learn, from experience, what matters and what is important. If we are looking for an alternative to practical induction, it cannot, therefore, be a method that learns from experience. Practical induction allows us to learn our way around new domains as we enter them; a technique that does not must evidently come pre-equipped for all possible domains of human decision making. This might seem like an overly strong requirement; after all, why can't we just get by on what we have? But any domain of human decision making that is not new now, was new at some point in the past. So if a non-inductive technique is shown to fail in new domains, we will also have shown that it cannot have worked in the old. I will return to this family of issues below; in the meantime, we have a second constraint on what an alternative to practical induction can look like.

We have a third constraint already put in place by the arguments of Chapter 2: we cannot, in one way or another, just make up our practical judgments as we go. If we do this, we will be putting ourselves in the position of having assumed backward-directed inferential commitments that it is obvious we cannot meet; that is, it will be apparent to us that we have no real reason for having the practical judgment that could underwrite whatever practical conclusions we might consider drawing from it. So addressing a conflict between two competing practical judgments by simply deciding that, henceforth, one will be the weightier of the two will not work, and neither will just inventing a bridging practical judgment.

We can embody these constraints by imagining that a suitable supply of agency-supporting practical judgments is to be had through the interpretation of a holy text. Consider the Talmud, a compendium of rabbinical legal proceedings that is presented as exegesis of the word of God. The Talmud provides a good deal of general guidance on day-to-day decisions of many kinds, and is a plausible source of somewhat general practical judgments that might be used in determining the defeasibility conditions of one's practical syllogisms; and it is presumably sufficiently consistent with itself to ensure that adhering to its dictates would not by that very token undermine unity of agency. Now I suspect—in fact, more than suspect, for reasons I will come to in the next section—that the Talmud is by no means free of the results of practical induction. And I also suspect that there are many areas of life (particularly modern life) for which it does not give a great deal of guidance: aerospace technology development, for example. As we have just seen, these characteristics make the Talmud an unsatisfactory alternative to practical induction. So let us imagine these difficulties surmounted by a Talmud-like work. The *Super-Talmud* is produced entirely through exegesis of a document supposedly the word of God, and so is free of the taint of practical induction.[2] (It might be that the word of an omniscient and benevolent God would be bound to anticipate the results of practical induction, even if He does not Himself need the inference technique. I am going to assume, for purposes of argument, agreement between the interpreted word of God and the results of practical induction to be entirely coincidental. As we will eventually see, a good deal of this assumption can be discharged.) Because it is derived from Scripture, its adherents do not worry that their backward-directed inferential commitments have not been met. And the Super-Talmud is far more thorough than the actual Talmud, covering pretty much every area of human life and decision: when the time comes to choose which of several propulsion technologies one should sink one's development money into, the Super-Talmud will have something to say to this—as to every—issue.

The Super-Talmud is a representative member of the class of possible substitutes for practical induction. If it cannot provide the practical judgments we need to make unity of agency possible, then we have no alternative to practical induction, and we must accept it as legitimate. Now perhaps we would not do well if we used the Super-Talmud; perhaps we would miss out on those things whose value we could only learn from experience. But is there any reason to think that one way in which we would do poorly would be by having our unity of agency undercut?

---

2. If interpretation involves the principle of charity, and if application of the principle of charity relies on the results of practical induction, then interpretation normally, and perhaps necessarily, is tainted by practical induction. I will pretend, for the sake of the argument, that interpretative practices that do not presuppose the use of practical induction are possible.

§ 4.2

Practical induction is observed to work. When I turn up at my favorite cafe for cappuccino and the Sicilian Sandwich, I expect that because it was pretty good the last many times, it will still be pretty good. And, usually, it is: I eat my sandwich, drink my coffee, engage in animated conversation, and prove to have made a reasonably good choice of lunch spot.[3]

Suppose, however, that one day I turn up at the Cafe Nefeli and the particular practical judgment I form of my coffee and sandwich is not in line with my inductive generalization: in mid-bite I realize that my sandwich might as well be crawling with small revolting insects. (Perhaps this is because it *is* crawling with small revolting insects, or perhaps it is because, although the sandwich appears to be superficially the same, my reaction to it has somehow changed.)[4] The food is vile and inedible; unable to swallow even the mouthful I have, I lurch, gagging, from the cafe. When this happens, my plans for the day will have to be changed. I will have to find lunch somewhere else, or do without lunch. I will have to contact Michael and tell him not to look for me there later. And certainly (here is practical induction resolutely at work once more) I am not going back there: I will need to find a new cafe to frequent. In

---

3. One might be tempted to use this observation, and others like it, as the basis for a practical-inductive proof of the principle of practical induction, modelled on the various attempts to prove inductively the principle of traditional, theoretical induction: Induction has often worked in the past, so I infer, inductively, that it will continue to work in the future. (For a discussion of this strategy, see Braithwaite, 1953/1974.) Analogously, particular practical inductions have proven to be a good idea, time after time, so I generalize inductively, and infer that practical induction is a good idea. This, however, is a temptation I will resist; I mean rather to use the fact that practical induction works to frame an exploration of what happens to unity of agency when it does not.

4. One issue that might be thought to crop up at this point is whether there has to be a descriptive or factual difference, if there is an evaluative one. (Could my sandwich be in every physical way the same, but now be revolting?) That may or may not be the case: I don't want to engage the metaphysical question now. What matters is that whatever 'factual' differences there may be inferentially unavailable to me. Often I do not know what physical changes have occurred within the sandwich (or within myself); all I have to go on is the evaluation.

short, counterinductive surprises entail the sudden readjustment of one's plans.

The temporally extended aspect of unity of agency involves the continuity, across time, of one's plans and policies. At most stages of one's life, one normally has a good many plans underway and policies in force, and there is a good deal of cohesiveness among them; this means that they can assimilate a moderate amount of readjustment without occasioning what would look like a breakdown in continuity of the practical self, since any readjustment takes place against a relatively stable background of concerns, intentions, and so on.

But a relatively stable background of concerns, plans, policies, and so on is only possible if unpleasant (or for that matter, overly pleasant) surprises of the kind just described are the exception rather than the rule. If, almost every time I attempted to execute a plan, I found myself forming particular practical judgments that prevented me from going through with it, I would end up rarely following through on my plans. (In such circumstances I would almost certainly perform the second-order practical induction, and conclude that making plans and embarking on actions was just not worth it. This would mean simply *giving up* on agency, an eventuality resembling cases of extreme depression. Because my agency cannot keep going without my participation, the failure of practical induction would in this way as well result in the disintegration of agency.)[5] A life consisting of plans uniformly disrupted and policies always violated is not a single continuing life at all, and the creature who inhabits it is something less than a temporally extended agent.

Now for this breakdown in practical selfhood and unity of agency to be avoided, my practical expectations must be realized sufficiently often. That they are realized often enough is to be explained as follows. My past practical judgments have formed a pattern from which I am able to generalize, and because practical induction is reasonably effective, when I do generalize in this way, I am not unduly surprised. None of this is to say that our world might not have been such as to frustrate practical

---

5. For a recent survey of the closely related phenomenon of learned helplessness, see Peterson et al., 1993.

induction consistently and favor some other strategy;[6] and none of it shows that practical induction will not stop working tomorrow. But, as our relative success in forming and carrying out plans witnesses, we are lucky enough to live in a world in which practical induction works enough of the time.[7]

We can now see what is wrong with the Super-Talmud (and how different it must be from the actual Talmud). Recall that we are supposing that any overlap between the practical judgments supplied by the Super-Talmud and those supplied by practical induction is a rare coincidence. Any actual scheme of practical judgments that people are able to live *by* must be informed, by practical induction, of what people are able to live *with*. If the Super-Talmud is not so informed, and if it gives guidance on enough of the domains in which decisions are required of us, then its followers will be constantly facing inedible sandwiches and like surprises. Because they take their backward-directed inferential commitments to be met (the Super-Talmud is, after all, thought to be the word of God), we can suppose they do their best to stick with its dictates. But because they are not able to go through with the plans and policies they adopt, they will end up in more or less the same boat as we would be in if practical induction one day stopped working at all: which is to say, they would not manage to amount to unified agents. (In a bind like this, anyone

---

6. Although it has been argued that if any non-inductive strategy works, induction must work too, since one can induce on the success of the non-inductive strategy. (See Salmon, 1974, p. 86.) If this argument could be adapted to practical induction, it might follow that if the world were such as to consistently frustrate practical induction, then it would not favor a different strategy in its place.

7. What this means is that we are not just *committed* to the usability of practical induction: we are the best possible evidence for it, since if it did not work, we would not be here. Because this point is something of an aside, I won't provide the argument or qualifications needed to make it stick; here, instead, is a thumbnail sketch of the reasons for it. If one is now deliberating about what to do, then one is a temporally extended agent: in order to be in a position to deliberate, it is necessary to have something of a past. And this means in turn that if one is now deliberating, one has extremely good evidence that practical induction has been working: after all, if it had not, no one would be *there*. To be sure, that practical induction has been working is no guarantee that it will keep on working. But that it has been working well enough so far makes the supposition for which I have been arguing, that it will continue to work, far more reasonable than it would otherwise seem.

but a fanatic would give up on the Super-Talmud rather quickly; doing so for the obvious reasons, however, would be an exercise in practical induction.)

If the diachronic unity of agency presupposed in deliberation is disrupted by an alternative source of the practical judgments needed to support synchronic unity of agency, that would-be alternative is thereby shown to be unsatisfactory. It is of no use to be able to integrate your present practical judgments into a process of deliberation resulting in a plan of action, if the way in which you do this makes it inevitable that you will be unable to follow through on your intentions. Alternatives to practical induction will undercut practical unity of the self over time.

§ 4.3

The ways in which the Super-Talmud undercuts diachronic unity of agency have synchronic relatives. The Super-Talmud was introduced as a source of the somewhat general practical judgments needed to mediate between the major premises of conflicting practical syllogisms; and we supposed that the pronouncements of the Super-Talmud agreed with those of practical induction only rarely and coincidentally. But, as I remarked earlier, our empirical characters—the layers of evaluative response that we bring to bear on practical problems facing us—are to a large extent the accumulated deposits of processes of practical induction.

If this is right, we have further reason to expect the Super-Talmud to be a poor substitute for practical induction. The deliberative success of an agent using the Super-Talmud will depend on whether its deliverances are able to get the different considerations already in play to engage one another, and they will be able to do this only if there is a certain amount of common ground between the Super-Talmud's take on the domain in which the decision is being made, and the agent's. But we have no reason whatsoever to suppose that there will be this common ground. Because there is no coordination between the different sources of practical judgments in play, the likeliest occurrence will be the dictates of the Super-Talmud weighing in as additional competing considerations, rather than mediating links; that is, they will make the problem harder rather than solving it. (They may, of course, prove to be utterly irrelevant to the concerns at hand.) Here is an illustration.[8]

> Carol is wondering whether to use the extra money in this month's budget to buy a futon or to pay off the IRS. The bed she now has creaks at night, and she doesn't want to lose any more sleep over it. On the other hand, there are penalties for non-payment of back taxes, and she doesn't want to lose any more sleep over that, either.
>
> Uncertain which to do, she consults the Super-Talmud; unfortunately, the Super-Talmud's pronouncements on the subjects of taxes, budgeting, and sleeping arrangements have to do, respectively, with the first fruits of the crop, financial numerology, and the ritual purification of the bedding. They are on-topic—the Super-Talmud, after all, has entries for all possible areas of human agency—but entirely at cross-purposes to Carol's concerns. When Carol looks at the tradeoff she is facing, she sees issues of personal convenience; when the Super-Talmud looks at the same tradeoff, it sees issues centering on the separation of the sacred from the profane. The Super-Talmud accordingly makes her problem harder, rather than solving it: now she needs to worry not only about the financial costs of a good night's sleep, but about the sin of sleeping beneath unblessed blankets; and she still does not know which of the two kinds of sleeplessness is to be dealt with first. Because they fail to connect the motivations she already has, the pronouncements of the Super-Talmud cannot underwrite the defeasibility of her practical syllogisms.

When practical induction is focused on a domain of human endeavor, it tends to produce practical judgments that fit together and interlock. I am not going to speculate here as to why that is so, since the question is of a piece with other problems I mean to circumnavigate: whether practical induction can be guaranteed to work, which attempted practical inductions are likely to work, and so on. (The theoretical analog of the question would be: why is it that empirical investigation of a domain so often results in a theory of that domain, rather than a collection of scattered and unconnected observations and rules of thumb?) There is of course one way of taking the question that admits of an easy

---

8. I'm grateful to Tamar Laddy for the example.

answer: a putative domain of which this was not the case would, probably, soon cease to be a domain of human endeavor, either because people would avoid it, or because it would fail to be recognized as a single region. Be that as it may, this tendency suggests that if practical induction is so often successful in supplying practical judgments able to mediate and connect the elements of practical syllogisms with their potential defeaters, this is because the premises of those syllogisms are usually, directly or indirectly, themselves the product of practical induction.

The argument to this point suggests, first, that even if the Super-Talmud were able to underwrite synchronic unity of agency, it would do so at the price of disrupting the agent's unity over time. What is more, if the agent has a history of relying on practical induction—as we all do—then the Super-Talmud is unlikely to be able to underwrite synchronic unity of agency, either.

§ 4.4

The Super-Talmud seems to be an unworkable substitute for practical induction because, for agents like ourselves, mismatches are bound to arise between the Super-Talmud's pronouncements and various practical judgments that such agents cannot but have. Evidently, there are two possible ways of addressing the problem: bringing the agent's practical judgments into line with the Super-Talmud, and bringing the Super-Talmud into line with the agent's practical judgments.

Consider the first of these options: Recall the problems that arose in Carol's case when she attempted to use the Super-Talmud to mediate between practical judgments derived from an entirely different source. This problem would have been avoided had Carol's original motivations been shaped by the Super-Talmud itself; the Super-Talmud failed because it was not being used consistently. Just as Orthodox Jews try to raise their children to have motivational outlooks that conform to the Talmud, so we must imagine the adherents of the Super-Talmud brought up to have motivational outlooks informed, not by practical induction, but by the Super-Talmud. If Carol has been raised on the Super-Talmud from the very beginning, then perhaps her practical problems will be couched in terms of the conflicting demands of piety—and maybe she will even sleep soundly in a creaking bed if she knows she is lying between ritually pure sheets. Perhaps a similar strategy will also allow us to preempt the ruptures of diachronic personal identity that we have been considering. If the Super-Talmud provides me both with the criteria I use to choose my cafe and sandwich, and with the criteria I use in evaluating them later on, I can be spared agency-disrupting surprises. If I have been brought up to choose the cafe because it is kosher, perhaps I can also have been brought up to gag when I believe myself to be eating an unkosher sandwich, but not otherwise.

Imagine, then, setting out to make the Super-Talmud the sole source of motivating reasons for these extremely devout individuals: the major premises of such an agent's practical syllogisms—that is, the practical judgments that the deliverances of the Super-Talmud are to mediate between—are themselves to be pronouncements of the Super-Talmud. Imagine also that the Super-Talmud is to control the agent's reactions to the situations he encounters, which we have seen is necessary to avoid the disruption of the agent's unity over time. Taken together, these expedients would remove the mismatch between an agent's practical judgments and our candidate alternative to practical induction, by reshaping the agent to fit the alternative. How successful is such a project likely to be?[9]

Not very. Both recent and not-so-recent history suggest that it is not at all realistic to expect that an arbitrary ideology will be able to reshape its subjects in this way. The twentieth century has seen several large-scale attempts, notorious for leaving no expedient untried, to educate populations into this or that ideology. But the bright-eyed Stakhanovites portrayed in the Socialist Realist murals never existed, because, despite countless hooks and crooks, it proved impossible to create them. Such failures are very good inductive evidence that attempts like these do not

---

9. If all, or almost all, of the agent's practical judgments derive from the Super-Talmud, we may start to wonder whether the putative agent is really a locus of agency at all, rather than a tool or toy of the real agent (in this case, God or the Borgesian document standing in for Him). By contrast, even when practical induction supplies a preponderance of the agent's somewhat general practical judgments, the agent does not seem to disappear. I think the reason for this is that accumulating the results of practical induction is also part of the process of constructing a unified agent: the agent is on the scene both as the one doing the construction, and as its result.

work, for roughly the reasons we have just canvassed: there turn out to be things you just plain can't stand, or can't give up, or simply don't like, or turn out to like anyway—or to which the proposed practical judgments seem blankly irrelevant. No matter how thoroughly you are taught, say, the virtues of socialism, and that economic equality matters more than the material and political inconveniences that are its price, you still may not be able to put up with what turn out to be more than just inconveniences; and even economic equality itself may be much less palatable than it seemed, once you finally get it.

The popular way of describing these failures is as unsuccessful attempts to change 'human nature', and it is important to see both what this locution gets wrong, and what it gets right. First, let's use it to recast the objection that practical induction has not been shown to be indispensable because it has not been shown that there are no usable alternatives to it. The recast objection concedes that an *arbitrarily* selected ideology, one that takes no account of human nature, is almost bound to instruct its subjects to perform actions that are outside the range of what human beings can bring themselves to do; and because internalizing the ideology will fail to remove resistance to it, the upshot will be fractures in the practical unity of the self. (Think of the Christian experiment with asceticism, its elaborate vocabulary of temptations, struggles, weak-willed sinners, and the like—and the way it was ultimately forced to a gradual moderation of the stringency of its demands.) But this means only that the author of the Super-Talmud needs to take human nature into account. An alternative to practical induction should not deliver itself of just *any* more or less consistent set of practical judgments. Viable alternatives to practical induction need to be designed to conform to human nature, and perhaps also to the psychologies of the individuals for whom they are intended. That is, we are now considering the second of the two options broached at the outset of this section: removing the mismatch between the agent and the Super-Talmud by adjusting the Super-Talmud to fit the agent's practical judgments.

But how is one to learn about 'human nature', if not the way we normally learn about it, that is, if not by practical induction? We learn what we can tolerate by practical induction, both our own and others'. We learn what makes life go well for us by trying things out and generalizing from what we find. The history of political failure that we adduced as evidence for the intractability of 'human nature' is equally evidence for its inscrutability. It is at least an empirical fact—and, in the next chapter, I will argue that it is not *just* an empirical fact—that we have no way of finding out what we would have to know to design a usable Super-Talmud that does not involve practical induction, in one guise or another; and if that is right, then this apparent avenue out is also a dead end.[10]

If practical induction *is* the way we learn about these things, then 'human nature' is a misleading name for what we are learning about. The suggestion implicit in the term is that when I conclude—through what is evidently a practical induction—that warm, friendly, and open smiles are delightful (where this is to be thought of as a judgment with practical content), I am not actually learning something about some smiles. Rather, I am learning something about *myself.* I do in fact discover, the suggestion will go, that I am disposed to respond with delight to some smiles, and I discover this by encountering smiles and generalizing; but what I am generalizing about is my own reactions. (The reactions of other individuals, cultures, and species may be very different, which

----

10. It might be objected that scientific advances, perhaps just around the corner, are going to change this. So let's consider briefly what would be involved in such an advance. If the author of the Super-Talmud is to know what its adherents will be able to put up with, he will need to anticipate their responses, and since practical induction is off-limits to him, we can require that he be able to anticipate responses to types of situation that have not been encountered before. (Since he can't have learned from experience, all situations, from the practical point of view, might as well be previously unencountered.) Now how a person is going to respond to new circumstances is an empirical question, so prediction will require an underlying constancy of some other kind; that is, prediction will involve induction, but not practical induction. Staying within the spirit of the objection, but without, I think, loss of generality, let's take the underlying constancy to be physical. So, it will be suggested: (1) We can inspect the physical workings of the human organism. (2) Psychological states, and so, practical judgments: (a) supervene on the physical workings, and what is more, (b) can be inferred from them. (3) The physical workings of the organism in psychologically unfamiliar circumstances can be predicted. (4) And so the responses of human beings to specified but hitherto unencountered situations can be predicted.

To review the status of the claims composing this train of thought: (2a) is a widely held dogma that I will not contest just now; but (2b) does not follow from it, and—when it is labeled reductionism about the mental—is as widely rejected. In the next chapter I will give reasons for rejecting (2b) and (3).

goes to show, it will be further suggested, that what I am really learning about is myself.) And if what I am learning about is myself, or human nature, then in principle I could replace practical induction with self-examination, or a study of human nature.

This suggestion, incidentally, fits very nicely with the instrumentalist's way of seeing the problem. On the instrumentalist view, what I am primarily learning about, when I find open and friendly smiles to be delightful, is my desires. (Presumably, that I desire to be smiled at in certain ways.) I could just as well have arrived at the same conclusion in any of several other ways. I might have imagined the smiles, and introspectively observed my own affective response;[11] or I might have been told by an observant friend (or therapist) that I want to be smiled at; or I might, as happens in philosophical science fiction, literally have had my head examined.

But this way of seeing things is misguided, and we can see why by looking at practical judgments side by side with judgments about secondary qualities. Although accounts differ, secondary qualities can be picked out as those properties that have to be understood in terms of the internal structure and dispositions of observers. The textbook example is the property of being red: red things are red because we're built to see them that way, and because, under normal circumstances, we do see them that way. (Other creatures might see different colors.) The parallels between practical judgments and secondary qualities are extensive; perhaps this is because practical judgments, or some of them, actually *are* judgments of secondary qualities: this would help explain the ways in which practical judgments vary from person to person, for instance.[12] But these parallels should make the proposed substitution of self-examination for practical induction seem extremely far-fetched. Is it plausible that when I learn that some category of object is red, I am

---

11. The widespread notion that one can learn about the moral or practical world by exercising one's imagination in this way should seem on the face of it to be an extremely odd idea. The most charitable way to make sense of it is to attribute to the method's practitioners the thought that all there really is to know about the moral or practical world amounts to facts about the ways in which agents are built.

12. See McDowell, 1985, Wiggins, 1991, pp. 189–199, McGinn, 1983, pp. 145–155, Stroud, 1989. For background discussion, see Mackie, 1976, Dennett, 1991, pp. 369–411.

learning not about that category of object, but about *myself*? And is it plausible that I could therefore bypass observation and generalization in favor of some kind of self-examination, and learn instead what colors different kinds of things are by studying myself—say, through some kind of imaginative exercise of the kind just described? It is hard to imagine a more unrealistic view.[13]

§ 4.5

The Super-Talmud is a dummy alternative to practical induction, and one likely response to the argument built around it is skepticism that the more familiar proposals surveyed earlier on, and others like them, would really prove to have the same shortcomings. Here I cannot, of course, give the old favorites the lengthy treatment to which they have become accustomed. But it is worth indicating how the considerations deployed against the Super-Talmud apply to them as well.

I remarked earlier that appealing to empirical character—to just being the way one is—will not serve as an alternative to practical induction, because the way one is is largely the result of practical induction. But there is another, very important reason why empirical character will not do the job. People flatter themselves in thinking that their personalities contain resources that would allow them to meet just about any situation they might face with something better than flailing, and it is perhaps this confidence in the ampleness of those resources that disposes them, every so often, to defend their choices by insisting that that is just the way they are. (I will not try to decide when that is a good reason, and when it is merely self-indulgence unbecoming in an adult.) But, because there is no such thing as getting something for nothing, this self-congratulatory attitude is undeserved: there is just not enough empirical character to go around. Empirical character fails to meet the second condition we imposed on the Super-Talmud; it does not equip one to cope with all, or even more than a very narrow range, of the possible domains of human activity. (Given how quickly character runs out, it is just as well that human life is not routinized enough for one to get by on it: a life so sunk

---

13. I will say a little more about why it is unrealistic in section 5.4.

in a rut as to be navigable entirely through habit, impulse, and prejudice is scarcely a life.) The limits of empirical character provide another way of explaining why attempting to anticipate the results of practical induction by investigating human nature, or the personalities or characters of agents, is a non-starter. When we consider what is there within (rather than what practical induction will someday perhaps reveal to us without), we see that there is not all that much to investigate.

With the exception of simply picking exceptionless rules or overriding ends arbitrarily (and this strategy, recall, fails to meet the third constraint, that of allowing us to assume the backward-directed inferential commitments those rules or ends would require), the items in our survey, like empirical character, borrow a good deal of their plausibility from a concealed reliance on the results of practical induction. The hedonist principle of always aiming at the greatest amount of pleasure is not simply outlandish because we know, from our own practical experience, that pleasure does matter. (Whether we understand why it matters is another question, and one that I will return to in Chapter 6.) Kant's requirement that one never lie tallies, at least somewhat, with the results of practical induction: very often, at any rate, we find dishonesty to be a bad idea. (I do not mean to suggest that this finding is properly thought of as merely prudential.) It would be naive to suppose that principles like these are, whatever their proponents may allege, the products of pure a priori reasoning. If adhering to them does not produce immediately fragmented agency, it is because practical induction is behind the scenes and is doing the real work.

But once they are ensconced as general, a priori guides to action, they turn out to work only as long as the practical inductions on which they were based do. It is all very well to have determined that honesty is not just the best, but the only policy; but if, on the one hand, you plan to tell the truth, and, on the other, start finding yourself in situations where you cannot go through with it (perhaps where, you realize, telling the truth is the morally repugnant easy way out), then, if you cannot draw inductive conclusions and change your policy, your plans will go nowhere. If you have nothing to go on but the pursuit of pleasure, even once you find it to be an intolerable bore, sooner or later you will not be pursuing much of anything.

A very similar point tells against coherentist policies as alternatives to practical induction. If coherence is construed as other than merely a form or ingredient of practical induction, then modifying one's system of practical judgments so as to increase its coherence will, surprisingly, erode unity of agency rather than augmenting it. Because, sooner or later, my plans and policies are going to need revision, increasing the mutual coherence of my decisions, plans and policies will ultimately make the required revisions more rather than less drastic. The Kantian variation on this theme illustrates the point nicely. I may think that I can intend to treat all cases similar to this one just as I mean to treat this one, and I may think that it would be fine by me if others followed my example. But the only way to find out if I really could, and if it *would* be fine by me, is through practical induction; one simply does not know, without practical induction, whether, to use the jargon, one can will one's maxim to be a universal law. Coherence alone—or the Categorical Imperative alone—are not enough. They may or may not be part of the armory of rationality, but if they are, they can work only in tandem with practical induction; they are not an alternative to it.[14]

I have been assuming that a practical principle that does not itself invoke practical induction will not produce results that are sufficiently coordinated with those of practical induction to be workable. But one could imagine such a principle. By way of analogy, think of the truths of arithmetic. One might discover them inductively, or one might derive them from the Peano axioms; and one might expect the deliverances of the two methods to agree. Why should preestablished harmony of this kind not be found in the practical domain as well?

Such a principle might exist; after all, given the results of practical induction, and given their exhibiting sufficient systematicity, one could construct the principle from the results. But practical induction is the only way to know which of the very many possible principles the right principle is.

---

14. I remarked in Chapter 1 that expected utility theory is sometimes treated as a technical reformulation of instrumentalism. It is also sometimes treated as a kind of coherence theory, the idea being that one should adjust one's preferences to conform to the constraints they must satisfy if one is to have a well-defined utility function. When it is appropriated in this latter way, the point I have just made applies to expected utility theory as well.

§ 4.6

Let me quickly summarize the progress of our argument. We were considering removing mismatches between what the Super-Talmud tells an agent to do, and what he can bring himself to do, by tailoring the Super-Talmud to his proclivities. But if discovering those proclivities involves practical induction, then the Super-Talmud is not an alternative to practical induction at all. These mismatches cannot be removed either by getting the Super-Talmud to fit the agent, or, we saw earlier, by getting the agent to fit the Super-Talmud. Now the Super-Talmud was introduced as a representative member of the class of putative alternatives to practical induction; the images the name evokes may be colorful, but the argument has appealed only to general constraints on alternatives to practical induction, and to very general facts about human agency. If that is right, then an alternative to practical induction, applied to agents like ourselves, will not augment unity of agency, but will, rather, undercut it. And if *that* is right, there is no alternative to practical induction.

We saw that we are, in the course of practical deliberation, authorized to suppose that we are, now, synchronically unified agents, continuous with future selves who will execute our plans, and that those future selves will be sufficiently unified agents. We saw that synchronic unified agency requires a source of somewhat general practical judgments that can be used to mediate between the major premises of competing practical syllogisms, and that therefore we are authorized to suppose that such a source is at hand. We saw that the source from which we actually obtain these practical judgments is practical induction, and that were practical induction not accepted as a legitimate source of practical judgments, we would be unable to carry out our subsequent plans. And we saw that there are no alternatives to practical induction available, because would-be alternatives undercut, rather than support, unity of agency in beings like ourselves.

The upshot is that practical induction is legitimate, in that we are authorized, when we are deliberating, to assume that it works: that is, that it produces results we are licensed to use in practical deliberation. But this means that we are authorized to use it in the course of our practical deliberations; and this is all the legitimacy to which a pattern of practical reasoning could ever aspire.

5

When Sex and Drugs and Rock and Roll Are Not Enough

I have argued that the links between the usability of practical induction and our ability to sustain unified agency are tight; and with this conclusion in hand, the argument proper for the legitimacy of practical induction is over. However, even though we have all the pieces in place, we haven't yet seen why they fit. The argument has been tracing the convoluted topography of human agency. It's time to stand back and see why human agency has the topography it does.

Given the way we are built, we have no alternative to practical induction. (This is what talk of 'human nature' turns out to get right.) But why are we built that way? The argument I have just completed relies on a number of facts about human agency; for example, I argued that using the Super-Talmud would undercut unity of agency over time because human beings react to their circumstances by forming practical judgments—often very strong ones—about particulars in those circumstances. Now some of these facts are part and parcel of the larger fact that we *do* use practical induction. Human beings arguably have the capacity to form practical judgments when they are faced by particulars because they rely on practical induction; after all, if one is built to learn from experience, one had better have a way to take particular experiences into account. But a creature that did not use practical induction would not need to have such reactions, and might well not have them.[1] The argument seems to show that if we are built to use practical induction, we will have to use it; but it does not explain why we should have been built that way in the first place.[2]

Let me emphasize that this is not a gap in the argument we have just finished. Practical induction is not just something we *do;* it is something we have to do. We cannot give up practical induction for the Super-Talmud in the way that a commuter might take the subway instead of his car. The question of how one should think is a practical question, and for practical purposes, this is enough. We were trying to show that an agent must accept the legitimacy of practical induction in the context of practical deliberation, because he must suppose that he is a unified agent, and will remain one through the execution of his plan, and because supposing this means supposing that practical induction is a usable form of inference—which just means acknowledging the appropriateness of using it when he is trying to figure out what to do. But the agency that must be supposed unified is not that of some bare, abstract acting being; it is his *own* agency that he must presuppose. And so if the agent is human, by showing that, for human beings, there are no available alternatives to practical induction, we have shown that the agent must accept it as legitimate. The argument shows that practical induction is necessary, in the only sense of 'necessary' that matters here. It does not, however, show *why* it is necessary.

§ 5.1

Why is practical induction really necessary? Practical induction is learning, from experience, what matters. Learning from experience is necessary because one cannot come to the world already knowing what one will turn out to need to know. The problem is not, or not only, that there is too much to be known; it is not just a question of quantity or

---

1. Similarly, we saw in section 4.3 that the Super-Talmud fails to support unity of agency at a time because we already have a repertoire of practical judgments that is largely the product of practical induction.

2. I'm grateful to Sarah Buss for pressing me on this point.

bulk. Rather, it has to do with what is and is not already around to be known.

If the nature of the contents of the world never changed, then learning—or, at any rate, the learning of generalities—would eventually be over. And in that case there would be something to be said for the strategy of relying entirely on a body of received wisdom—a final edition of the Encyclopedia Britannica, in the theoretical domain, or a Super-Talmud, in the practical. But things do change. There is no fact more basic than the pervasiveness and persistence of genuine novelty. Ecclesiastes was just plain wrong: there *is* something new under the sun, almost all the time. And so there is too much to be known because there is always something new to know. This is why we have to be able to learn.

One can imagine worlds in which novelty is hard to come by. Readers familiar with the history of Artificial Intelligence may remember the Blocks World program, which developed and executed plans for moving colored blocks, pyramids, and balls in a very simple simulated space. Notice that it would be easy to equip a creature meant to live in the Blocks World with a short list of interests that would suffice to underwrite agency in any situation it could encounter.[3] This would be possible because the Blocks World contained only a few types of object, because the ways in which these objects could be combined were quite restricted, and because the Blocks World agent had available to it only a small number of possible actions.[4]

----

3. The Blocks World program did not do this; the program's planning processes were uniformly triggered by user commands.

4. Winograd, 1972. For a description of the Blocks World, see pp. 117–123; for a sample dialog, with commentary, see pp. 8ff.

It is worth underlining just how simple the Blocks World was. Because it was "designed less as a realistic simulation of a robot than to give the system a world to talk about" (p. 6), the tabletop world, 1200 units on a side, contained only 6 generic types of object, only one of which had more than one possible instance. There were three shapes, five colors, three primitive actions. (User defined colors were, however, possible.) Although the simulated robot was said to have an eye, even very basic features of perception, such as what would be visible to the eye, were not modeled: information about the objects in the world and their relations was simply maintained in a database. (This approach is of course only possible when the world is about as simple as this one.) And all events in the world were actions taken by the robot.

Our world is very different from the Blocks World. Our world does not come given as a set of primitive objects or predicates. It does not come as a small number of types of situation made up by combining primitive objects or predicates.[5] Novelty is one of the deepest and most important ontological features of the world. New kinds of things and never-before-seen properties come into being on a regular basis. And so we cannot avoid being confronted by unprecedented situations that contain unprecedented objects and require for their apprehension unprecedented concepts. And because, in novel situations, new things matter, and matter in ways that cannot be anticipated, the novelty with which we are faced is inescapably practical.

These are strong and frankly metaphysical claims, and I am not going to argue for them here. The larger argument, for the legitimacy of practical induction, is complete without the complicated and delicate discussion that would be necessary to defend them. (Complicated, because it would have to engage many other questions, regarding, e.g., supervenience and counterfactuals; delicate, because it's difficult to construct tight, general arguments about items whose shared characteristic is being unpredictably different.) Instead, I want only to show how the pervasiveness of novelty explains the observed features of human agency that the argument proper depends on. (To the extent that inference to the best explanation is a successful pattern of argument, doing that can be taken as the beginning of an argument for the metaphysical claim.)

Describing genuine novelty, and the new ways of mattering that accompany it, is a delicate matter as well. Newness has a very short shelf life; even if I were inventive enough to think up new and untold wonders, they would not long stay new and untold. So to illustrate the claims I have made as to the pervasiveness of novelty, I will use *past* novelty. Past examples have the disadvantages of hindsight: familiarity seems like obviousness, and it becomes hard to imagine that anyone could have failed

---

5. Physicalist reductionists, and some of their supervenience-preoccupied philosophical descendants, sometimes seem to have a view in which it does. But if one treats the ontology of contemporary physics as the alphabet our world is written in, one must not then have an impoverished sense of what that alphabet can express. To understand the combinatorial possibilities of an alphabet is not to have preempted literary innovation.

to see things as we do. So I ask the reader to bear in mind that what is now familiar was once not only not obvious, but often literally inconceivable.

There is a shortcut to appreciating the connections between new circumstances and novel interests. By and large, our interests cannot far outrun our concepts, and our concepts cannot far outrun the circumstances for which they are invented.[6] Think of the concepts devised to make sense of a culture, unimaginable even a century ago, that revolves around the automobile: commute, carjacking, beltway, drive-thru, the Great American Road Trip, gridlock, designated driver, speed trap, mileage, emissions standards, back seat driver, two car family, road food, whiplash, convertible, used car dealer, jackknifing, alternate side of the street parking, cruise control, lemon, flat tire—and the list has been barely started. Now think of how we have come to have interests and concerns given in terms of, and dependent on, these concepts. Once not so long ago, the exhilaration of taking the back roads in a convertible sports car would have been unintelligible; the awfulness of having to change a flat in the middle of the highway could not have been appreciated; and, as the failure of urban planning over the past half-century demonstrates, the long-term effects of automobiles on cities, neighborhoods, and communities—and consequently, on what people's attachments to them can reasonably end up being—were unforeseeable.

Here is another example. Although punctuality is among the chief modern virtues, it has not been much discussed by philosophers, presumably because it is not on the traditional philosopher's list of virtues, which dates back to Plato and Aristotle. Its absence from that list was inevitable. Before the reorganization of social life around the clock, completed only in the nineteenth century, hours had variable and vague lengths, and minutes were an astronomer's notion, useless in everyday life; there was no such thing as agreeing to meet for coffee at 8:45, or, more generally, a day made up of identical units of time, spooned out

---

6. Let me emphasize that 'by and large'. I want to allow that we do have interests about which we are unable to be articulate. But, as the example I am about to give indicates, for the vast majority of our interests, to have them does go hand in hand with, or at most one or two paces ahead of, our being able to articulate them.

one after another, to be allocated to one use or another, saved or wasted. Punctuality could not matter in anything like the way it matters today, and the ways in which it has turned out to matter could not have been imagined, prior to the transformation in temporal sensibilities, with anything amounting to a likelihood of accuracy.[7]

Let me take the opportunity to move onstage two reactions that I have found cases like this frequently prompt. The first, which we can call the *I-could-have-thought-of-that response,* has it that the concepts I have just inventoried were not, even while there was no call for them, in principle inaccessible: it was always possible to imagine—that is, to think sensibly—about the automotive or the chronometric world. The second reaction, which we can call the *nothing-new-matters response,* is that the practical side of novelty does not go all the way to the bottom. In this spirit, a utilitarian, for instance, might insist that, whatever the surprises that awaited in the world of the automobile and the clock, we knew, or could have known, that what was going to matter about them was the contribution they would make to human happiness, or to its converse. We already know, the utilitarian might continue, that we are not going to learn that anything but happiness really matters, and that we are not going to learn that happiness sometimes does not matter, or does not matter anymore, or matters differently than we had thought.[8] All there is to be surprised about are the differences clocks and cars make to people's happiness. It should accordingly be possible, with enough imaginative success on the theoretical side, to figure out what is going to matter in a novel situation. These reactions are important because they express a very common overconfidence in the powers of the imagination, one which, I will later suggest, is the mainspring of a misguided method of philosophizing, in moral theory and elsewhere, and they need to be kept firmly in check.

The philosophical conditioning these reactions represent is not something that can be undone all at once, though I will work at it over

---

7. See Dohrn-van Rossum, 1996, for a recent history of the social changes triggered by the development of the clock.

8. I'm grateful to Hilary Bok and Holly Smith for pressing me on these points.

the course of this chapter and the next.[9] In the meantime, notice that the record does not show that imagination, in either its theoretical or practical uses, lives up to the expectations these reactions involve. So-called Old Wave science fiction provides a wealth of attempts to anticipate the cultures and concepts that crystallize around new technology. This genre was tightly controlled by John Campbell, editor of *Astounding Science Fiction* from the 1940s through the 1960s. Campbell prized technical accuracy and rigor in thinking through the consequences of change—so much so that narrative, character development, and other literary desiderata often seemed to be little more than window dressing for Campbell-approved thought experiments. Reality has caught up with some of those attempts, and, almost without exception, they are embarrassingly wide of the mark. Most important for present purposes, when it came to predicting the practical demands novel circumstances were to make on us—that is, the interests and concerns we would properly come to have in them—the consistent pattern of failure is striking. Science fiction of the 1950s was populated almost exclusively by people whose interests and priorities are now recognizably those of the 1950s. The nothing-new-matters response piggybacks on the I-could-have-thought-of-that response, and when it comes to the latter, the proof of the pudding is in the eating: while the I-could-have-thought-of-that response is quite natural, what empirical evidence there is tells us that you could *not* have thought of that, after all.

The nothing-new-matters response is misguided for a further reason: it forgets its own past. The concerns it takes for granted—for instance, those that traditional moral theories have been built around, such as even-handedness, virtue, happiness, and the like—are themselves the product of the very process we have been examining. An empty, lifeless universe would be one in which nothing much mattered; and our universe was, once upon a time, empty and lifeless. In a world that originally contained no life at all, and then only life for which interests of this kind made no sense, new domains opened themselves up one after another; in the then radically novel sphere of social animals, and eventually,

---

9. For further discussion, see Millgram, 1996.

human beings, phenomena such as fairness, happiness, and character became possible, and became appropriate objects of practical attention. We
are in the position of being able to take it for granted that certain things
matter only because, in our own past, it was not true that nothing new
mattered; and if it has happened these many times, it is very likely to
continue to happen. New human domains will appear that cannot be ne-
gotiated using only the practical guides to earlier domains. Note that it is
not just that the inventory of available concerns is supplemented in the
course of such transitions; just as, in the now not-so-new human world,
fairness can override the appetites for eating and mating that, let's suppose, dominated the world of the pre-social animals, so, in future new
domains, older priorities may be circumscribed, or overridden, or dis-
placed entirely.[10]

§ 5.2

Philosophers have not paid sufficient attention to the fact of
novelty, and, in particular, they have not thought through the practical
problem of how to take the world's surprisingness and originality into
account. How should we go about addressing this problem? Practical
problems can be vicariously one's own. We can adopt the point of view
of a designer who is considering how to construct a creature able to
function in a world permeated by novelty, and that is what I propose
to do now. Ought such a creature to incorporate practical induction in
its design?[11]

---

10. If I am right about this, then achieving completeness in a moral theory from the top
down is a pipe dream. Think of the best case: a moral theory related to its basic principles
in more or less the way arithmetic is related to the Peano axioms. From within, the theory
may present the appearance of completeness, just as, from the Peano axioms, it might
seem as if you could learn everything you needed to know about arithmetic. Now recall
that the next situation you find yourself in might be one in which arithmetic is not going
to do you a lot of good.

11. I want for now to bracket worries about this shift in standpoint. (There are often
overlooked limitations to what can be learned by projecting oneself into a designer's
point of view; I discuss some of the difficulties of drawing conclusions about rationality
from this kind of exercise in Millgram, 1991, sec. 5.) For present purposes, it suffices
that the argument proper for the legitimacy of practical induction does not depend on
adopting this standpoint.

What would happen to a creature that did not use practical induction in our novelty-rich world? Because it is hard to see what is going on when the examples are as complex as the cultural transformations produced by the clock and the automobile, let us imagine we have built a very simple creature of this kind. Since the creature will not learn from experience, it must come from the factory equipped with a set of interests and concerns that determine its assessments of situations, options, and so on.[12] We will, at the outset, assign it only four interests, to which we can give labels: Sex and Drugs and Rock and Roll. The creature acts only to advance these interests, and its experiences do not make it adjust these interests in any way.

Unfortunately, our creature will not be a particularly effective agent in many environments. Suppose we send it to College, a new environment of which the relevant features are two. First, in College, Sex and Drugs and Rock and Roll are not in short supply; our creature will have all it can handle, almost regardless of what decisions it makes. Second, in College, the creature is faced with large decisions that have only the most tenuous connection with its interests; for example, it must make choices among—to use matching labels—Courses, Majors, Extracurricular Activities, and Student Organizations. Strictly in terms of its interests, it does not really make a difference what the creature decides to do. And so it will fail to live up to the practical demands of the situation it is in: it will fail to decide, or decide badly, or decide in ways that fail to project coherent plans and patterns of action into its world. Once it gets to College it will cease to be a functioning agent.

Now if the creature does not care about the choices it has, why should it matter what decisions it makes? To raise this question is to let go one's

---

12. We have seen that such a creature must not have the on-the-spot reactions that, in humans, undercut plans not formed on the basis of practical induction; it must be incapable of being practically surprised. When it considers a situation in which it might find itself, its practical assessment of the anticipated situation will be the same assessment it will arrive at when the situation is at hand. (Of course, it may be surprised *theoretically;* that is, it may discover that the facts are not as it had thought. And in that case it may have to alter its practical assessment of the situation at hand. But its new assessment is the one it would have ideally arrived at in advance, had it been informed of the relevant facts.) Human beings are not immune to surprise, but since we are designing this creature from scratch, we can allow it to differ from us in this respect.

hold on the vicariously adopted point of view from which the question of what desires the creature has is part of a design problem. The point of practical reasoning is to guide action. The practical abilities of such a creature will give out whenever it finds itself in circumstances where its interests and concerns do not guide action; in these circumstances, its desires are inadequate. Desires are part of the toolkit of practical reasoning; they exist for the sake of practical reasoning, and not, as the widely held view has it, the other way around.

Four interests is an extremely small number of guiding lights. We might try to improve our creature either by expanding the number of its interests, or by choosing for it interests that are pervasive—that is, interests that will serve to guide action in every, or almost every, situation in which the creature might find itself. A little reflection on what pervasive interests might be shows that the latter strategy is unlikely to work. Plausibly pervasive interests and concerns—happiness, success, pleasure, even the altruistic aim of bettering the world—will not substitute for practical induction, because one needs to learn, as one encounters new kinds of situations, what success, happiness, and so on would *be,* in a situation of this or that kind—and these lessons turn out to be *practical* lessons, which we can learn only by practical induction. It is all very well to say that what is going to matter about automobiles or clocks is the difference they will make to people's happiness, but there is in the end only one way to find out whether happiness is a perfectly scheduled day, or misery, the daily commute, and that is to try them out and see how they go.[13] Because the creature we are designing is meant to be a creature that does not learn its priorities from experience, it cannot fill out its conception of a pervasive interest in this way.

Consequently, if our fabrication is to be a successful agent, we must make the list of its interests longer. How much longer? When we sent our creature to College, we were picking an environment in which its

---

13. See section 6.7. Interests that seem like exceptions do so, I think, in virtue of what amounts to unintentional equivocation: pleasure, for example, if thought of as a sensation, does not require learning, but is also not pervasive; whereas pleasure understood in a way that makes it plausibly pervasive is no longer a sensation. We will return to the subject of pleasure in Chapter 6.

interests were an inadequate guide to action. The reader is invited to try the thought experiment of inventing, for any given list of less-than-pervasive interests, a situation of this kind: it is easy enough to do, and what we can do, the world assuredly can do, if only because we are part of the world.

If novelty is as basic a feature of the world as I have been insisting, then we will not be able to anticipate the practical needs of the creature whose design we are considering. Even if we imagine ourselves omniscient with respect to our creature's vicissitudes in any given type of situation, we will need to anticipate *all* possible types of situation. And here we see that we could not produce the requisite list, because no finite list will do. Recall an earlier expository device, the Super-Talmud. The job we have taken on for the creature to whom we are imagining playing God is just that of writing a Super-Talmud for it. Recall also that we had to allow the extravagant supposition that the Super-Talmud included a volume for each of the possible domains of human decision and agency. Now if there are, as I have been claiming, always freshly-minted domains of human activity, then no finite edition will do. The Super-Talmud's alleged author was God, and it turns out that God had better be the author of the Super-Talmud, because no lesser being could do the job.

This point has two immediate upshots. The first is that the task of designing an agent that can cope with novelty without learning from experience is just not possible, since even if we, or God, could somehow specify the interests it must have, that specification could not be incorporated into the design of the agent. One volume of the Super-Talmud is heavy enough; a finite creature cannot be required to carry around with it a greater-than-finite number of volumes. The second is that we now have one way of explaining why it is we cannot anticipate the practical responses of agents to new circumstances—a precondition, we saw, of composing a usable Super-Talmud. If we cannot so much as inventory the situations that would prompt those responses, we are not going to be able to complete a survey of the responses themselves.

If we want our creature to be able to cope with the novelty in its world, we will have no alternative to equipping it with ways of learning its interests from experience. Practical induction is necessary for creatures who have to be able to respond intelligently to real novelty, and human agency is built around practical induction because we are creatures in this predicament.

§ 5.3

I have been arguing that the legitimacy of practical induction is to be explained in terms of the part it has to play in a successful strategy for coping with a world in which there is always something new waiting around the next bend. But it might be objected that using practical induction cannot be required of a successful strategy, because there are apparently successful strategies that do not use it. Bacteria, ants, oysters, and redwood trees do not seem to learn new interests from experience; dogs, pigeons, and many other animals learn little. If redwoods do not need practical induction, why do we?

This is a convenient occasion to insert a reminder as to the scope of the claim for which I have been arguing. I have attempted to show that, if one is going to engage in practical deliberation, then one must treat practical induction as a legitimate form of practical reasoning. But I have not attempted to demonstrate anything about non-deliberative modes of agency—or, if the term 'agency' is to be reserved for deliberatively unified planning creatures like (sometimes) ourselves, about beings that proceed without thinking about what to do first. Human beings differ from bacteria, ants, and so on, in that human actions are often, directly or indirectly, the upshots of practical deliberation. If you are not going to try to *figure out* what to do, then you do not have to try to figure out what to do using practical induction.

That said, we can add that there is less to the success of non-inductive design strategies than meets the eye. Other-than-inductive strategies, even when they do not allow the agents that embody them to learn new interests and concerns themselves, do generally manage a crude imitation of practical induction, by having natural selection teach its lessons, the slow and hard way, to populations rather than to individuals. The slow and hard way of learning these lessons may be adequate in the pre-human world. But it is far less so in a world that seems to be becoming more and more a human artifact. Novelty was frequent enough before human beings came on the scene, but it comes thicker and faster the more say people have in how the world is arranged. By the time natural selection gets around to letting the redwoods know that it is time to change their ways, the last of them will be gone; the redwoods are, so to speak, a clear-cut case of the failure of non-inductive strategies. (This is, to be sure, a double-edged example: if it shows that the redwoods are not learning quickly enough, it is also an example of our inability to change our collective priorities sufficiently rapidly on the basis of our own experience.)

§ 5.4

The importance of novelty explains not only our being organized to learn our priorities from experience, but many of the details of that organization. I have already remarked that our ability to be brought up short by experience is part of the package—that in order to learn what matters from experience, we need to make practical observations of the particulars in it. Other aspects of human agency that our argument has exploited also fall into place around the challenge of being prepared for novelty.

Perhaps the most central of these is the defeasibility of the practical syllogism. It is characteristic of genuine novelty that the ways in which it will have to be taken into account cannot be anticipated; something that is different from anything you have seen before may make a difference you could not have imagined. This means that any general practical rule may have unforeseen, and realistically unforeseeable, exceptions. So it is a mistake to treat defeasibility as a threat against which one might armor oneself by looking for exceptionless principles: an apparent counterexample to the pervasiveness of defeasibility cannot be known to be anything more than a rule whose defeating conditions are too original to have been anticipated, and too tardy to have already forced themselves on our attention.

Whether or not there are practical principles that would turn out to have no exceptions, we cannot wait to find them. Practical reasoning must rise to the occasion; it cannot be put on hold till the end of time. Because just about any practical reasoning worth doing will involve considerations of some degree of generality, we must proceed to reason with general (or somewhat general) practical judgments that we realize may well run into circumstances for which they are unsuited. So we are forced to adopt the strategy of affirming our practical judgments on the one hand, while treating them with a certain tentativeness on the other; we make inferences from them, but keep an eye out for conditions in which they will turn out not to apply. In short, the only compromise we can make between the power of novelty to overturn our expectations and the requirement that our practical inferences be timely is the defeasible practical syllogism.

Novelty explains not only the fact of defeasibility, but the ways we handle it. Novelty of relations is entailed by novelty of relata. When we introduce a new kind of element into an already familiar territory, the ways in which the new element is important vis-à-vis the different kinds of already familiar items in the territory will have to be figured out one by one.[14] The practical relations in which novel items stand to other items in the territory are themselves to be expressed as practical judgments—in fact, the connecting practical judgments we encountered earlier, when we were considering the ways the possibly defeating conditions of a practical syllogism are taken into account. Because these connecting practical judgments are also novel, no merely routine method of arriving at them can be counted on; this is why any attempt to square the ways in which newly juxtaposed items matter that does not depend on experience will, almost always, be no better than a guess. This, in turn, is why conflicts between somewhat general practical judgments have to be resolved *ad hoc;* and it is why the resolutions so often depend on practical judgments inductively arrived at. It is also why the strengths of desires

---

14. Of course, practical syllogisms are defeasible by familiar as well as novel considerations; let me mention two reasons for this. First, if we think of the familiar territory as having been built up by introducing novel elements into it one after the other, then, even if each exercise of figuring out how the new kind of element matters with respect to an old kind, or group of kinds, takes a fixed amount of time, exhaustively investigating the lot would take 2^n such exercises. Because the problem is intractable, it cannot have been solved for any reasonably populous territory; and so novelty will remain in combinations even when items taken singly are no longer fresh.

Second, once it is in place, the strategy of defeasible reasoning has further benefits. If we are prepared to reason with piecemeal premises, trusting to our own alertness to catch impending errors, we can keep our repertoire of practical principles far more manageable than it would otherwise be.

are so sketchy. Strengths of desires encode judgments of relative importance; when an item is novel, you probably do not understand how it is important, and so a judgment as to its relative importance is not a judgment you should have made.

Recall our earlier thought experiment of designing an induction-free agent. I focused before on the impossibility of assembling a sufficiently exhaustive list of interests for it, given the variety of situations in which it might find itself. But we can now see that there is the further difficulty of anticipating what will matter for our creature in each type of novel situation it is to encounter. When, in our roles as designers, we consider novel situations, we must be able to figure out, in advance, what aspects of that situation will make a difference to the creature on our imaginary drawing board; and as any engineer will testify, this kind of thing is nearly impossible to ascertain without experiment.[15] We saw that we cannot supply our creature with the entire Super-Talmud, because it has too many volumes; we can see now that we will not even be able to do a decent job of writing the individual volumes in the set.

Some time back, while discussing a comparison of practical judgments to secondary quality judgments, I stated that it was unrealistic to expect to be able to predict either an agent's secondary quality judgments or his practical responses to novel situations, simply by studying the agent.[16] We can now explain why: the secondary quality judgment is the upshot of an interaction between the 'primary qualities'—the properties that can be understood in terms other than those of an observer's structure and dispositions to react to them—of the agent and its environ-

---

15. The recent history of the American space program is a nice illustration of this point. Because trying things out in space is extremely expensive, a good deal of thought and effort—measured in hundreds of millions, and occasionally in billions, of dollars—is put into constructing devices that will work first time through. Now space is a relatively simple environment: it is mostly empty, and the behavior of objects in it can be cleanly modeled using well-understood physical theories in a way hardly possible elsewhere. Nonetheless, even in this best-case domain, the record has been dismal: Mars Observer, which vanished; Galileo, unable to deploy its main antenna; Clementine, accidentally out of fuel; the Hubble Space Telescope, whose famously defective optics are perhaps less to the present point than the solar panels that turned out to vibrate once in orbit; and, of course, the generally erratic performance of equipment taken up on the Space Shuttle.

16. See section 4.4.

ment. In novel situations, one really has no idea how the two are likely to interact; and typically, one does not know what the relevant 'primary qualities' in the novel sitation are. It is a mistake to think that there is a description of, for instance, the underlying physical system that is both complete and usable. And so it is a mistake to think that the description in terms of 'primary qualities' comes first, and can be used as a short-cut to predicting the 'secondary qualities' in novel circumstances. On the contrary, it is only by experimenting in the novel circumstances, and seeing how the agent responds, that we can determine what the correct description given in terms of 'primary qualities' would be.

We need, finally, to consider an objection I mentioned early on, that the effectiveness of practical induction is at bottom simply the effective-ness of traditional, theoretical induction. Once again, I do not need to resist the suggestion that I have shown a single pattern of inference, in-duction, to have a practical as well as a theoretical domain of application. But it is necessary to counter the suggestion that practical induction can be *reduced* to theoretical induction. That suggestion proposed factoring a putative practical induction into, on the one hand, a fully theoreti-cal induction, and on the other, instrumental reasoning proceeding from a desire matching the conclusion of the theoretical induction. (In our earlier example, the conclusion of the theoretical induction was a gen-eral view about the taste of hot polenta, and the matching desire was for something that tastes like *that*.) Because the reductionist objection holds that it is always possible to decompose instances of practical induction in this way, it assumes two burdens: that of producing a purely theoretical inductive conclusion capable of interlocking with the posited desire, and that of producing a desire capable of interlocking with the conclusion of the theoretical induction.[17]

---

17. It is at least an open question whether the first of these burdens can be successfully shouldered. When the conclusion of the practical induction to be reduced is expressed using a 'thick ethical concept'—that is, a concept with both descriptive and evaluative dimensions, such as 'sleazy' or 'courageous' or 'delicious'—there seems some point in tackling the tricky task of producing the corresponding purely descriptive predicate used in the alleged theoretical induction. (While it is not usually possible to say, in different words, what the descriptive dimension of a word like 'sleazy' or 'delicious' is, generat-ing the descriptive component by muting the evaluative force of the 'thick' concept is

But now that we can see what practical induction is *for,* it is clear that those desires are not there to be had, and that if the reductionist objection were right about what practical inductions came to, they could not do the job for which we need them. To reiterate, the proposed factoring of practical induction into theoretical induction and instrumental reasoning requires the agent to have available desires whose objects match the conclusions of his theoretical inductions. (Having realized that hot polenta tastes like *this,* I must have a desire for something with this taste, if the effect of the practical induction is to be recaptured.) Now I have been claiming that we need practical induction because of the way in which new and unanticipated domains of activity open themselves up to us. In these new domains, we cannot be expected to have guiding desires of the degree of generality requisite to organize our plans, decisions, and actions. After all, we have had no opportunities to come to have them. So when a theoretical induction in a newly-opened domain concludes, there will be no matching desire waiting to meet it. And so, instead of forming plans and policies that project coherent patterns of agency into the barely explored sphere of activity, we will simply be brought up short. The proposed reduction of practical induction will not work because it will not leave us with a method that works; and we have already argued that we can, while we are deliberating, take ourselves to have a method that works.

What seemed like an unprincipled list of brute facts about human beings has turned out to delineate the necessary contours of any being facing, with some chance of success, what looks to be an unavoidable cognitive task. While the argument extending over the last three chapters has leaned toward the baroque, there is a very simple idea underlying it. Our world is full of new and surprising things. The only way to come to understand how they matter for us is to let experience teach us. That is why we have to use practical induction.

---

arguably a legitimate technique—although the question is controversial. For a critical survey of the literature on thick ethical concepts, see Millgram, 1995a.) But when its conclusion is expressed using a 'thin' concept (like 'good', 'ought', or 'right'), there seems to be no space to insert the theoretical concept the objection requires. (We will see in the next chapter why the most promising candidate will not do.)

6

How to Keep Pleasure
in Mind

I have argued that practical induction is a legitimate form of practical reasoning, and that it must work often enough if we are unified agents, which we must, within the context of practical deliberation, take ourselves to be. But this conclusion raises a further question, regarding the premises of practical inductions. We cannot take the conclusions of our practical inductions any more seriously than we are willing to take the practical judgments that serve as their premises; so where do the premises of practical inductions come from? In the terminology of Chapter 2, one's forward-directed inferential commitments must be matched by backward-directed commitments; so the premises of practical inductions themselves involve suitable backward-directed inferential commitments. How can we understand these to be met?

We can begin by asking where traditional, theoretical inductions get their premises from. Sometimes, of course, their premises are produced by other inferences, inductive inferences not least among them: Newton's Laws were inductively arrived at on the basis of, among other things, Kepler's Laws, which were in turn the upshot of inductive reasoning.[1] But passing the buck to other inferences just defers the problem: if we proceed backward in the chain of inferences, if human finitude precludes an infinite regress, and if circularity in the chain is not an option, then

---

1. Recall that by 'induction' I mean not just induction by enumeration, but inference from instances to covering generalizations, and that theory construction and selection are being counted, for present purposes, as of a piece with inductive inference.

we will eventually bottom out in premises that are not further justified.[2] This suggests that practical reasoning must bottom out in what one cares about, or thinks is important, for no further reason—that is, in something tantamount to brute desires. And if this is the case, how can *any* account of practical reasoning do better than instrumentalism?

The premises of theoretical inductions, however, are not just the products of further inferences: they come from observation and testimony as well. In this chapter and the next, I'm going to argue that both have practical analogs; on the assumption that we take testimony seriously in part because we can suppose it to be backed up by observation, I'll discuss practical observation first.

§ 6.1

The suggestion that there is such a thing as practical observation might be met with incredulity. Am I proposing that we have as-yet-unnoticed senses, over and above the usual five, for perceiving practical matters? And if I am, what causal mechanisms could impress what must evidently be values (consequently not facts, consequently not causes) on the practical sense?[3] But I am, of course, proposing no such thing, and to think that arguments along these lines are needed would be to get hold of the wrong end of the stick. Rather, the sense in which we need to show that practical observations can be taken seriously is just this: there are practical judgments of particulars, formed in response to, and reflecting, experience, that can be legitimately used as premises in practical inductions.

---

2. The circularity option is usually called 'coherence' by its proponents. Whether coherentist justification can be made to work in either the theoretical or practical domain is an open question; Millgram and Thagard, 1996, advances a family of techniques for investigating it. For reasons discussed in section 4.5, I do not think that coherence can replace the category of premises I am now about to consider.

3. Compare Mackie, 1983. Although the objection is likely to be raised in this form—and so is worth mentioning—this version of it is not actually available. Recall from the introduction that, because the metaphysics of value is to be read off the correct account of practical reasoning, the fact-value distinction cannot be invoked at this point. I will develop the objection, in a way that avoids this misstep, in section 6.6.

Now the argument for *this* conclusion is already on hand. Over the last three chapters, I have argued that practical induction is required for unity of agency, and that consequently we can, while deliberating, take it that practical induction is a legitimate pattern of inference, and that it works often enough. So if there is a category of particular practical judgments that must function as practical observations in order for practical induction to work, then, just as we are licensed in the course of practical deliberation to proceed on the supposition that practical induction is effective, so we are similarly licensed to proceed on the supposition that judgments in this category can be legitimately treated as observations.

So the task at hand is not so much to advance a new argument, as to fill out and give substance to this one. Granted that we must deliberate on the assumption that there is something amounting to practical observation, and that it is both common enough and effective enough to support unity of agency, like many a philosophical existence proof, this argument will not be persuasive if we are unable to recognize practical observation in our ordinary lives. Accordingly I need, first, to provide an account of practical observation that will allow us to identify it in common and commonplace experience, and thereby to forestall the worry that believing in practical observation is distant from common sense. Second, with the identification in hand, I need to explain how practical observations differ from the instrumentalist's desires.

I am going to claim that the hallmark of much, if not all, practical observation is pleasure. I'll proceed by identifying an element of practical observations, which I will call "pleasure". Then I will argue that this element *is* pleasure. In addition to filling in the account of practical induction, I will use the discussion of pleasure to provide a new argument against hedonism. I'll address an objection that has been pending since Chapter 2, to the effect that desires can be controlled by modifying one's tastes, and say something about what it takes to be an observation, practical or otherwise. Finally, I will draw conclusions regarding, first, the recently popular proposal that practical reasoning can proceed by more tightly specifying vaguely conceived ends or rules, and, second, the methods appropriate to substantive moral theory.

§ 6.2

We can best approach the role pleasure plays in practical observation by beginning with examples. Here is one borrowed from the experience of an acquaintance:

> Diana works for a company that provides and maintains indoor plants for offices. Faced with a tree that was almost completely defoliated, she decided to try to bring it back to life, rather than go to the expense of replacing it. She pruned it back, cleaned off the dead material, watered the tree carefully, and applied rooting hormone. Soon she was receiving compliments from people on the site for *other* plants; the care she was putting into the tree was carrying over to the rest of the account, but she herself did not realize that this was happening until the compliments began. The tree, which had looked dead, revived, and "is today a beautiful tree".
>
> Diana describes bringing the tree back to life as having been "a big thrill". She says that meeting the challenge gave her genuine satisfaction: "it's really fun to see trees come back, go from bare branches to being covered with beautiful green leaves again." As she started to pay more attention to trees, her interest in them deepened: "As I saw trees grow into what I had cut, I started to enjoy it more and more, as I realized I could affect them in a long-term way. It's like doing sculpture in four dimensions." She has learned that she likes challenges that involve improving and reviving living things through her own perseverance, intelligence and skill; her next job will involve treating, nurturing, and learning about living things.[4]

There is a good deal in this example that deserves careful attention. First, Diana began her work on the dying tree for reasons that had nothing to do with the intrinsic rewards of caring for trees: she felt that an important part of her job was keeping expensive plant replacements to a minimum. Through her experience, Diana came to want to care for trees, and to have a more general desire for the challenges and rewards of bringing living things back to a state of health. That is, in the course

---

4. I'm grateful to Michelle Desaulniers for the example.

of the experience, Diana acquired new ends; ends, moreover, for which she was able to adduce reasons.

Second, central to the process was Diana's finding the challenge of reviving the dying tree to be *fun*. It called forth energy and concentration that overflowed to the rest of the account. She found herself enthusiastic about and engaged by what she was doing. We are all familiar with the feeling of our work (or other things) going well, eliciting our attention and energy in a way that makes a hard job seem almost easy. When one finds a task pleasant, one engages in it willingly, even eagerly; there is no need to force oneself to it, even when it is difficult. It is this feeling that I will call *pleasure,* and I will treat this kind of case as the central or paradigmatic instance of pleasure.

Let me pause a moment to say what I mean by 'feeling'. I am going to distinguish feelings from sensations, so in calling pleasure a feeling, I am not suggesting that it is a sensation; in fact, I am implying that it is *not* a sensation. On this way of speaking, sensations and the awareness of them generally go in tandem. Feelings, however, may be had unawares; a familiar example is the depressed person who does not realize that he is depressed. Unlike sensations, the feeling of pleasure may sometimes be recognized only in retrospect, or when one's attention is called to it by others. Feelings can of course involve sensations, sometimes in a way that makes it tempting to say that the sensations are part of the feelings; we often identify feelings by the sensations they involve (that sinking feeling). But feelings do not always involve the same sensations: a feeling of elation may be accompanied by a sensation of light-headedness in one case, by a sensation of butterflies in the stomach in another, and by no special sensation in a third. While pleasure often involves some sensation or other, there is no particular sensation, or class of sensations, that it necessarily involves.[5]

A third point to notice is that the conclusion Diana draws on the basis of her cumulative experience with trees amounts to a practical induction. This is an occasion to return to the instrumentalist objection, considered in previous chapters, that what is going on in cases like these

---

5. See Gosling, 1969, pp. 46f, and section 6.6.

is really theoretical rather than practical induction. Diana, the objection would go here, is out to attain pleasure, and learns inductively that certain things give her pleasure. Her decision to pursue these things is the conclusion of instrumental reasoning; now that she knows that tending trees is a way to get pleasure, she decides to tend trees. Diana hasn't acquired any genuinely new ends; she has learned ways to address an end she already had. I remarked earlier that the objection assumes the burden of producing an entirely theoretical conclusion to the entirely theoretical induction it claims is taking place;[6] being pleasurable is perhaps the most promising general-purpose predicate in terms of which such conclusions can be framed, and so it will be instructive to see why pleasure will not do the job. For now, notice how alien this construal of the case is to the first-hand description. What Diana wants to do is tend trees, which she has found to be pleasurable—not to obtain pleasure *by* tending trees. This is a subtle but real difference, one which it is not obvious that an instrumentalist account can reconstruct. We will in short order be in a position to explain the difference between wanting to engage in the pleasurable activity of tending trees, and wanting to obtain pleasure by tending trees.

Before I go on to the account of pleasure, let me offer an example of the use of its contrary, displeasure or unpleasantness, in practical reasoning:[7]

> Ellen[8] had been supporting herself as a waitress in New York while pursuing a dancing career. As she went from job to job, the time she remained in each grew shorter and shorter. Although she began each job

---

6. See note 17, section 5.4.

7. Although traditionally 'pain' has been used to mean the converse of pleasure (cf., e.g., Bentham, 1789/1973 and Mill, 1861/1969), I will use words like 'displeasure' and 'unpleasant' instead. In my view, while pain is generally unpleasant, many things are unpleasant but not painful. Further support for this terminological choice may be found in the fact that we need a name for the sensations we normally call 'pain'; but since pleasure is a feeling, rather than a sensation, its contrary should be a feeling as well. See below, notes 9 and 36; also Ryle, 1954, pp. 57ff.

8. Real name withheld on request.

with a good deal of enthusiasm, she would soon find things to hate about the job, would fight with the boss, and get fired.

Over the course of this period, she found herself ever more unable to cope with the day-to-day details of living. She was unable to pay her rent or run her errands; she wasn't getting dates; and at one point she realized: "I'm crying all the time, so I must not be doing the right thing." She describes the time as dominated by "a feeling of complete despair. I just couldn't do it. There were these basic things that very stupid people could do, that I couldn't do."

Although she felt miserable, it took a long time until she understood what was making her feel that way. Eventually she realized that while some things were going very badly, "the things that were good for me were going well and easily." Finally, on the first day of a new job waiting table, she quit. "I couldn't bring myself to do it. I didn't even get as far as taking the first order." At that point she was resolved not to waitress anymore. She now works for an architect and dances in the evenings.

If the central case of pleasure is the feeling that things are going well, that one is performing smoothly and successfully, and that difficulties are manageable and can be overcome, the central case of displeasure is the converse: one must force oneself to engage in the unpleasant activity, and going ahead with it is like pulling teeth. In extreme cases, one cannot cope, simple tasks become impossible, and doing what one is doing is unbearable.[9]

Again, one might suppose that Ellen's decision was taken on the basis of instrumental reasoning, the goal of which was to avoid displeasure. But this would misconstrue the example. Ellen herself describes her feeling of despair and dysfunctionality as telling her that she was doing

---

9. Examples like this one make understandable the traditional use of 'pain' as the contrary of 'pleasure': it is all too natural to describe Ellen's experience as painful. This is not simply a linguistic coincidence. The physical sensations of pain that are usually taken as the central cases of pain typically (although not always) make it difficult or impossible to continue doing what one is doing. When this is the case, physical pain occupies much the same role as the more central cases of unpleasantness that we are now considering. This fact explains why it is natural to extend the word 'pain' to instances such as this one, even when they do not literally involve pain.

something wrong. She distinguishes her choosing to avoid waitressing (which was unpleasant and even painful) from a possible choice which she denies having made, that of choosing to avoid displeasure and pain by not waitressing. This is a distinction that most of us can discover in our own experience. It is quite often the case that decisions that attend to pleasure and its contrary use them as signs or symptoms, evidence as to how well things are going. One then often chooses the more pleasant (or less unpleasant) option, but this is not because pleasure is one's goal: rather, pleasure is an indication of something else.

§ 6.3

We saw in Chapter 2 that even desires come with strings attached. One way to say what those strings are is to return to a point made by Elizabeth Anscombe, that desires involve desirability characterizations.[10] 'Desire' is no longer part of our preferred vocabulary, but the link remains when we replace the notion of a desire with that of a practical judgment. This is a consequence of the argument of the previous chapters: If inferences proceeding from a practical judgment are to be defeasible, they must involve some understanding of how its object is desirable; if you don't see why something is important, you won't be in a position to determine whether, in particular instances, it's more important than something else. And defeasibility, we saw, is required for unity of agency. So a practical judgment commits one to a view as to the desirability (or undesirability) of its object: that object must be taken to be desirable (or undesirable) in some way or other.[11]

Now what does being committed to something's being desirable come to in practice? There is a point that used to be made by coherence theorists, that one is never in a position to compare one's beliefs with the world as it really is: all one is ever in a position to do is to check

---

10. Cf. note 17, section 2.4.

11. The notion of desirability in play here is, again, a placeholder; see note 18, section 2.4. I will return to related issues in section 6.6. Notice that I am not claiming that one cannot find something desirable in one respect while failing to find it desirable in another respect, or even while finding it undesirable, all things considered.

whether one's beliefs stand in inferential relations of conflict, compatibility, support, and so on, with *other* beliefs that one has. Being committed to something's being true cannot in practice be manifested in anything beyond one's inferential commitments. And a very important part of these inferential commitments amounts to anticipating other beliefs.[12]

Let's see an illustration of this. Suppose I inform you that I believe that there is milk in the refrigerator. I am committed to the milk's in fact being in the refrigerator: if it is not there, I am wrong. I expect that if I go and look, it will be there. Now what does going and looking amount to? I put myself in appropriate circumstances (by walking up to the refrigerator and opening the door): in these circumstances, I come to have a belief that there is a carton of milk on the top shelf. This belief is a *rock-bottom* belief, that is, it is not inferred from further beliefs. I may or may not be able to give further reasons for relying on this belief, but the belief is not inferred from further reasons. It is clear that, on pain of an infinite regress, there must be such beliefs.

We can type this belief more tightly. There are rock-bottom (i.e., non-inferred) beliefs very different from this one: hunches or gut feelings, or the axioms of Euclidean geometry, understood the old-fashioned way, as self-evident truths. In contrast to these, the rock-bottom belief I acquire by looking in the refrigerator is *experiential*: I come to believe that there is milk in the refrigerator by looking in the refrigerator.[13]

A belief's being rock-bottom carries no implication of indefeasibility: no matter how observational my belief, I may later retract it. Also, a belief's being rock-bottom carries no denial that there are necessary conditions of its acquisition that must be described in terms of further beliefs. A good deal of background is typically required for coming to

---

12. I do not mean to suggest that believing that p does not commit one to p *itself* being the case, nor to claim that p's being the case must amount to facts about my present, future, or possible beliefs; I am not endorsing a form of verificationism. The words 'in practice' are meant to carry this qualification.

13. The 'by' in the last sentence is important: looking in the refrigerator might cause in some deviant way a rock-bottom *hunch* that there's milk in the refrigerator; I mean to pick out the class of cases in which one's belief formation is appropriately responsive to one's immediate experience. The distinction is familiar, if hard to articulate precisely, and I won't try to spell it out further here.

have a rock-bottom belief. For example, if I were unacquainted with milk cartons and their contents, my opening the refrigerator would not have led to my believing that there was milk in the refrigerator. Beliefs whose acquisition requires such background may be, nonetheless, non-inferentially acquired, and be accordingly rock-bottom beliefs.[14]

The commitment to *p*'s truth involves, in practice, the expectation that various beliefs, some experiential and rock-bottom, and some not, will be compatible with my belief that *p*. Now rock-bottom beliefs highlight a feature that beliefs have more generally. If my rock-bottom belief is impugned, I cannot fall back on the premises from which I inferred it, for what makes it a rock-bottom belief is that I acquired it non-inferentially.[15] In these circumstances, I may find myself becoming aware of a *feeling* (not a sensation) of belief, which I will call *a feeling of conviction*. "I just *looked* in the refrigerator. What do you mean, 'How do I know?' Of *course* I know." If I stop myself in the middle of such a tirade, the feeling I find there is typically a feeling of conviction.[16]

---

14. It may be argued that inference *must* have taken place, perhaps unconsciously; settling the question would involve thrashing out what counts as inference, and so whether the notion of unconscious inference in play here makes sense. I will instead just point out what I take to be a salient difference between inference and observation. Like inferences, observations are defeasible, but they are, at least most of the time, defeasible in a very different way. My observations are corrected in one of two ways. They may be corrected after the fact, as when I am informed that objects in the mirror are closer than they appear. (After I read the notice, they still appear farther away than they are.) Or they may be corrected by training my vision; in the practical case, by training my taste. (As I work with television commercials, I learn to see the stuff that gets poured on cereal as Elmer's Glue rather than milk; it now *looks* like Elmer's. And as it comes to look like Elmer's Glue, it ceases to seem appetizing.) Here I am, as it were, effecting an adjustment in the machinery ahead of time. It is much harder—though perhaps not impossible—to assimilate one's awareness of defeating conditions into the observation at run time.

15. I may be able to provide arguments from other (background) beliefs from which I *could* have inferred it; and sometimes I will actually fall back on these. The situation I am now interested in is one in which I do not fall back on further beliefs.

16. When asked to list one's convictions—the things about which one has this feeling—one normally produces, say, points of religious or political or moral doctrine, rather than beliefs about what's in the refrigerator. And this might suggest that conviction is rather rare. But I am claiming that conviction is a feeling, rather than a sensation, which is to say that one need not always be aware of it. One may be made aware of the feeling by a challenge; if someone exerts pressure on my claim to know where I live, I shall become

The feeling of conviction (or, I will just say, *conviction*) plays an important role in one's epistemic economy—particularly when it is of the rock-bottom, experiential variety. If, on considering a proposition, I find it unconvincing—if I lack the feeling of conviction—I may decide that I am on the wrong track (or that someone else is). If I do not feel conviction in situations in which I'm face to face with the object of my would-be belief (that is, when experiential rock-bottom belief is at issue), then it's going to be very difficult to convince me. And if in such situations I *do* feel conviction, my views on the subject will be difficult to dislodge. Seeing is, often enough, believing; experiential rock-bottom conviction is the familiar feeling that goes along with believing because you're seeing.

I now want to identify practical reasoning's analog of experiential rock-bottom conviction. I claimed that practical judgments involve commitments to desirability characterizations. But what do those commitments amount to in practice? Often, to the expectation that when one puts oneself in the appropriate situations, e.g., that when one actually gets what one wants, one will not be horribly disappointed and wish that one had never heard of it. Rather, one expects that when one gets it, it will *turn out* to be desirable. Now a primary indicator of whether something is desirable or not is pleasure. Pleasure is the rock-bottom judgment of desirability of an object of present experience (and likewise, displeasure is the rock-bottom judgment of undesirability, also directed toward present experience).[17]

Pleasure is not, of course, the sole indicator of desirabilty. Other indicators may be inferences, or rock-bottom judgments of desirability that, like hunches, are not experiential. It is therefore not the case that taking something to be desirable *entails* expecting it to be pleasurable, any more

---

aware of a feeling of conviction as deeply rooted as those attached to any of my political views. It is also often true that invoking one's feeling of conviction is a way of registering one's inability to articulate one's reasons for believing what one believes. (I'm grateful to Sydney Shoemaker for raising this point.) But, if my account is on track, this is just what we should expect. When a belief is rock-bottom, we fall back on conviction; so it is not surprising that we invoke conviction to signal the non-inferential origins of a belief.

17. I am leaving to one side the pleasures of anticipation, memory, and imagination. These require separate treatment.

than believing something entails expecting an encounter with the subject of your belief to produce conviction. I believe that the earth revolves around the sun, but, Wittgenstein's famous remark notwithstanding, I don't expect it to look that way. I may think the policies I support to be for the best, even though I expect that I will only see the unfortunate side-effects I know they will have. Judgments of desirability can be mistaken, and one can be mistakenly disappointed. There are—and as we will see shortly, it is important that there are—false pleasures. Magicians, pickpockets, and con artists know that both conviction produced by the evidence of one's own eyes and pleasure are fallible. That fact does not, however, make either dispensable.

Because feelings of pleasure amount to judgments of desirability, they need be no more self-centered than those judgments. Diana learned that tending trees was desirable for her; but she might, in taking pleasure at seeing trees tended by another, have learned that tending trees is desirable without qualification. Cynics use the pleasures of altruism and sympathy to argue that even altruism is selfish; I take these pleasures to show that the desirability pleasure tracks need not revolve around the first person indexical.[18]

It may sound peculiar to identify a *feeling* with a *judgment.* Possibly this is because one feels that there must be more to a judgment than a feeling; possibly because one can make judgments that do not feel like much at all. But recall that I am not using 'feeling' as a synonym for sensation: because it is not a sensation, a feeling is not precluded from having cognitive content in the way one might think sensations are; and, as I remarked earlier, one can have feelings of which one is hardly, or not at all, aware. I am avoiding distinguishing feelings from judgments because the distinction seems too forced here to be useful. But one can just as well think of these feelings as aspects or accompaniments of judgments.

---

18. Robert Nozick has suggested that emotions track values, that is, counterfactually covary with them (1989, pp. 96–98). Whether or not it is true of emotions in general, the account I am developing has it that something very much along these lines holds of pleasure.

§ 6.4

Practical reasoning tends to take one from a position of lesser pleasure to a position of greater pleasure. When I decide to make Korean scallion pancakes instead of another round of marinated tofu, the likely upshot is that my subsequent life will be more pleasant than otherwise. Some philosophers have noticed this tendency, and concluded that pleasure is one's sole and necessary goal. In this they could not be more mistaken. Hedonists err in roughly the way that someone who thinks that the goal of inquiry is to maximize conviction errs. Normally, one's inquiries tend to take one from a position of lesser conviction to a position of greater conviction: after the inquiry, one has more beliefs, and believes things more strongly. However—and this is very important—in general one's goal is *not* conviction: one's goal is truth. Conviction is epistemically important as a guide to truth, but conviction *per se* is not the object of my efforts.[19]

To conclude that because one tends to move to positions of greater conviction one's goal is the conviction, rather than true and relevant belief, would be seriously to misconstrue the normal case of epistemic endeavor. One's feelings of conviction guide one's changes of belief, but this does not make them one's goal. Hedonists assume that because desires and goals change in response to experienced pleasure and displeasure, these must be the actual goals. But this view is naive: pleasure and displeasure are indications and signs of desirability we use in determining what our goals should be. Diana did not become devoted to trees as a way of pursuing pleasure (if she were only interested in pleasure,

---

19. Four caveats. First, successful inquiry does not always take one to a position of greater conviction; Plato's early dialogues are a nice example of this. Second, not everyone agrees that conviction is not the proper goal of one's epistemic efforts; Peirce, 1877/1955, for instance, seems to take exception to this point. Third, there are those who *do* act as though conviction *per se* were their goal. Fanatics of various stripes evidently just want to *believe;* they will go to great lengths to attain a *feeling* of conviction, without too much regard to *what* they believe. (See Hoffer, 1966.) And finally, recall from section 2.4 that there is only so much work the invocation of truth can do before it degenerates into table-thumping.

she would not have genuinely cared about the trees); rather, her pleasurable experiences helped her decide that one of her ends ought to be tending trees. Ellen did not, she says, abandon waitressing in order to avoid pain or unpleasantness; rather, she took the pain and unpleasantness as an indication that waitressing was not desirable, and was not in itself worthwhile. Similarly, time spent with my friend is, by and large, pleasurable; and were this not the case, eventually we should cease being friends. Nonetheless, it would be a mistake to construe the friendship instrumentally—to conclude that I befriend him solely in order to obtain pleasure. The correct account of the counterfactual is, rather, this: if time spent together becomes, by and large, unpleasant, I shall start to wonder whether something is wrong with the friendship.

Although hedonism is a mistake, some degree of it is perhaps common enough, and there is another way to say what kind of mistake it is. Money is a device for representing value; like pleasure, it is important as an indicator of something else. Misers, perversely, take the indicator to be the thing of value; hedonists, just as perversely, do likewise. Notice that the argument not only cuts against egoistic hedonism, but against universal hedonism, or pleasure-utilitarianism, as well. If pleasure is a kind of estimate of desirability, the utilitarian's Good consists in maximizing the number and force of these estimates. This is a quite unlikely conception of the Good.

Earlier I claimed that it would be a mistake to construe Diana's change of mind as amounting to theoretical induction (i.e., about what produces pleasure) together with instrumental reasoning directed toward the goal of pleasure. We're now in a position to say just what is wrong with that construal.

Such inductive reasoning can of course take place: one can learn, as a psychological fact about oneself, that tending trees produces pleasure, in much the way one can learn that one can't help finding well-groomed and sincere-sounding young men with attaché cases convincing. But normally, the conclusion about what tends to produce pleasure is related, more or less directly, to the desirability of objects of pleasure. Now suppose that one is instead interested *simply* in the pleasure produced, and not in any further desirability the pleasure may indicate, and that one proposes to use the knowledge of what gives one pleasure to put oneself in situations that one will find pleasurable, without regard to the reliability of one's judgments of desirability in those circumstances. That would be a little like putting oneself in the way of a series of well-groomed and sincere-sounding young men with attaché cases, without too much regard to *what* they are likely to persuade one of, just in order to acquire *convictions*. It is evidence of the strategy's incoherence that knowingly putting oneself in the way of acquiring convictions in this manner will impede one's ability actually to acquire them. Similarly, if one puts oneself in situations where one expects that one's pleasure will fail to be responsive to actual desirability, one's ability to make the judgments of desirability in which pleasure consists will be corroded. (The realization makes pleasures seem hollow; and hollow pleasures are very soon no longer pleasures at all.) This suggests that acting on the hedonist proposal would end up giving you, not more pleasure, but less.[20] Fortunately for Diana, this is not what is going on in her deliberations; her reasoning is quite able to survive her own scrutiny, and that is because it is directed toward the desirability of tending trees, rather than her own pleasure.

In developing an account of pleasure that construes it as a guide to the choice of ends, rather than an end itself, we have addressed the problem of the provenance of the premises of practical induction. Seeing how pleasure works in our cognitive economy is seeing what practical observation can be like; and once we can recognize practical observation in familiar acts of judgment, the claim that there must be such a thing (or that we must proceed on the assumption that there is such a thing) should no longer seem unintuitive or difficult to accept.

Theoretical reasoning that did not attend to the world—say, solely deductive reasoning—would be useless. Thinking that matters has to be informed by the way things are. If practical reasoning is to be useful, if it is to matter, it too will have to be informed by the way things are. Instrumentalist views of practical reasoning allow the world to have its say only by determining what is a means to what; but this is not enough.

---

20. I am tempted to think that a partial explanation for the paradox of hedonism (that is, the fact that many of the activities we engage in could not yield pleasure if their goal were understood to be pleasure) may be found here. Cf. Sidgwick, 1907/1981, pp. 48ff.

Attention to the cognitive role of pleasure shows how the world is given a further say in practical reasoning. Practical reasoning is informed by something that can be considered the practical analog of observation.

§ 6.5

The objection likely to be pressed most strongly against the foregoing is this: what does what I am calling 'pleasure' have to do with *pleasure*? Because the purpose of discussing pleasure was to show practical observation to be a familiar phenomenon, this is an objection that we need to address; and my argument against hedonism depends on this identification as well. So I will try to show how the observationalist account of pleasure I have presented accommodates the insights that motivate competing theories of pleasure, as well as the objections that have been traditionally urged against them. Showing how those insights are accommodated by my account will show it to be an account of the very thing into which they are insights—viz., pleasure.

I have been developing the observationalist account of pleasure in opposition to the instrumentalist understanding of it, on which pleasure serves the function of an ultimate goal or end. The insight that makes the instrumentalist view seem plausible is nicely rendered by Anscombe. She remarks that "'It's pleasant' is an adequate answer to 'What's the good of it?' or 'What do you want that for?' I.e., the chain of 'Why's' comes to an end with this answer."[21] This point seems to support the instrumentalist or hedonist view in the following way. It is taken that the chain of 'Why's' is a series of requests for further goals. 'Why are you going shopping?' 'To get some more moong dal.' 'Why do you want more moong dal?' 'To make cucumber soup.' 'Why are you going to make the soup?' (And so on.) It is presumed that the final answer ('It's pleasant') states the final goal, and that the reason it terminates explanation is that there is no further goal.

On the observationalist account, however, while 'It's pleasant' does indeed terminate explanation, it does so in much the way 'That's just how it looks to me' terminates explanations in the theoretical realm. 'It's pleasant' more or less amounts to: 'In experiencing it, I find it desirable'.

---

21. Anscombe, 1985, sec. 40.

One is not adducing a further goal, but affirming that the goal one has just mentioned is desirable. Notice that there is no need, on this account, to force the locution into some other form like 'I get pleasure from it'. The instrumentalist, by contrast, needs to identify some further item (the pleasure itself), distinct from the thing in which one takes pleasure. (This may be part of the motivation for taking pleasure to be a kind of sensation.) Locutions that allow this distinction to be made tend to be strained, which is evidence that we do not usually need ways of speaking that will permit us to do this.

Anscombe continues the passage we just quoted: "a claim *that* 'it's pleasant' can be challenged, or an explanation asked for ('But what *is* the pleasure of it?')." An instrumentalist must explain just how the final answer ('It's pleasant') can be challenged, and he seems to have only two choices: the challenge could consist in a denial that pleasure is one's goal (not an option for the hedonist), or in a claim that the penultimate goal is not in fact a satisfactory or efficient means of attaining pleasure. (This latter is a very unlikely gloss on 'But what is the pleasure of it?') Perhaps the instrumentalist can find a way to account for such challenges. Whether or not he can, the observationalist account is able to explain the possibility of a challenge without difficulty or undue forcing. Just as 'I believe it because I can see it' can (in appropriate circumstances) be challenged by 'Well, you shouldn't', or, 'No, you don't', so 'It's pleasant' can be challenged by, 'No, it isn't', or 'Well, it shouldn't be': roughly, by claiming that it's not, after all, desirable, and that something has gone wrong with one's observation.

The observationalist account, then, accommodates the two insights most partial to the instrumentalist view. (The other is the already discussed fact that 'You wouldn't have chosen it if it weren't pleasant' is so often true.) But pleasure also seems plausible as a primary goal because it is closely connected with the good—closely enough to be identified with it, or confused with it. Anscombe, for example, criticizes the hedonist account herself, on the grounds that pleasure seems to involve a prior judgment about good.[22] John Stuart Mill famously equates happiness, pleasure, desirability and utility. Bentham calls utility "that property in

---

22. If I am correct, this is not quite right: the judgment is not *prior;* rather, the pleasure just is the judgment.

any object, whereby it tends to produce benefit, advantage, pleasure, good, or happiness," adding, "all this in the present case comes to the same thing."[23] There is a very close tie between the notions of pleasure, of an object of choice, and of what is good.

Being able to explain this tie is a demand legitimately made of an account of pleasure. Conveniently enough, this connection lies at the heart of the observationalist account. From the first-person point of view, they are tied together in just the way that p and 'I believe that p' are. First, a rock-bottom judgment of desirability immediately directed toward the experienced object—that is, on the present account, *pleasure*—just *is* taking it to be desirable. Second, one wants only what one thinks desirable, that is, what one anticipates will turn out to be desirable. But expecting something to turn out to be desirable is, usually, expecting it to be pleasurable.[24]

The roles of pleasure as a terminator of explanation, and as something supposedly invoked by all desire, have been taken as objections to construing pleasure as a sensation: as Anscombe remarks in one of her more authentically Wittgensteinian moods, "Pleasure cannot be an impression; for no impression could have the consequences of pleasure."[25] Nonetheless, philosophers have often been tempted to understand pleasure on the model of sensation. One motivation may have been the instrumentalist's need for a detachable, yet always available, goal. Another may have been linguistic reflex: we talk about something's *feeling* pleasant, for example, and feelings are often confused with sensations. And I think there is a further point. Pleasure seems subject to something like first-person privilege: who to know better whether and how the experience is pleasant than the experiencing individual himself? The experiencing individual *just knows*—he does not have to investigate, or find out, the way one must with other matters of fact. Traditionally, sensations were thought to be the home of this kind of privilege and of privacy, so it is not surprising that pleasure was assimilated to sensation.

---

23. Mill, 1861/1969, Bentham, 1789/1973, ch. 1, sec. 3.

24. There may be a flip side to this connection. Sometimes expectation determines perception. When it does, thinking something to be desirable may make it seem desirable when you get it: that is, may make it pleasurable.

25. Anscombe, 1985, sec. 40.

On closer examination, neither first-person privilege nor privacy has turned out to be nearly as philosophically robust as it used to be acceptable to assume. (The story is familiar, and I will not recount it here.) Nonetheless, what remains is accommodated by my account. Pleasure plays a role in many ways analogous to that of certain facets of belief. Now belief naturally carries with it a certain first-person privilege: the modest one of being able, usually, to know what one believes without asking or otherwise investigating, and to know how strongly one feels one's beliefs. (There is, of course, no claim of infallibility being made here.) The analogy should make it unsurprising that pleasure exhibits similar features.

It is often objected to sensation accounts of pleasure that it is too heterogenous to be plausibly taken to be a sensation. What, it is asked, do all the different pleasurable sensations—those experienced while skiing, while reading poetry, while dozing in the sun, and so on—have in common save the trivial property of being pleasant? As Aristotle noticed, there are diverse pleasures proper to particular activities and senses. This fact is a problem for a view that would identify a single sensation or quality as the objective of rational deliberation and action; for in what sense is pleasure a *single* objective?[26] Again, rather than consider whether advocates of sensation accounts can parry this objection, I will just note that the fact it adduces is accommodated comfortably by the observationalist account. What do all convictions have in common—what could they be expected to have in common—save the property of being convictions? Beliefs are very different from one another because what each belief is, is mostly a matter of what it is about; and beliefs may be about very dissimilar things. If pleasure is the practical analog of conviction, we should expect pleasures to be very different from one another, and to share only apparent desirability. This is why pleasures are so diverse.

Philosophers uncomfortable with sensation models of pleasure have often adopted adverbial accounts. These philosophers recognize that pleasure is normally experienced in the course of doing something, and they take pleasure to be something about the manner in which the activity is done. They are also aware of the close connection between pleasure

---

26. *NE* 1175a22ff; see Gosling, 1969, pp. 28–53.

and enjoyment—sometimes so aware that they identify the two. I do not wish to try to disentangle pleasure and enjoyment from each other here, and will just set down my agreement that they *are* closely connected. As Leonard Katz has pointed out, depression mutes both, and anti-depressant drugs restore the capacity for both. It would be extremely odd to find someone who enjoyed himself thoroughly, but was unable to take pleasure in anything, or conversely, someone who encountered pleasure at every turn, but enjoyed nothing.[27]

The adverbial view has its problems: It is hard to say just what it is that all pleasurable activity has in common. (Words like "exuberance" and "eagerness" turn up in what are correctly taken to be the central cases, but these are ill-suited to describe naps on a warm summer day.) And it is hard to explain the role of pleasure in justification and choice under this construal.[28] Once more leaving aside the question of whether adverbial views can be defended against these objections, note that on the view I am advancing it is clear why pleasure taken in activity seems relatively central. Not only do we make our rock-bottom judgments in the course of whatever it is we are doing, but our deliberative attention to pleasure will be most importantly focused on our activities: we want to know whether what we are doing is going well, and if we ought to be doing it; and so we pay special attention to the pleasure or displeasure we take in it. But there will be no adverb (save the uninformative ones, 'pleasurably' and, possibly, 'enjoyably') sure to characterize all pleasurable activities, for activities of the most various kinds may be found desirable.

Finally for now, some philosophers have understood pleasure as something that causes one to want to continue or to repeat its object.[29] This view too has its problems: there seem to be pleasures we would not want more of; and it is in any case hard to say how such a dis-position could function as anything like a reason for action.[30] But the present treatment of pleasure explains why, when something is pleasant, we usually want to keep it up: pleasure is, or is an aspect of, a judgment

---

27. Katz, 1986, p. 119.

28. For a fuller discussion, see Gosling, 1969, pp. 54–85.

29. Brandt, 1979, p. 40.

30. The point is argued by Quinn, 1993, Essay 12.

of desirability, and when something is desirable it often—although of course not always—makes sense to want more of it.

It should now be far more plausible that when I say 'pleasure', I mean *pleasure*. The apparently incompatible motivations of competing theoretical views of pleasure are jointly accommodated by the account developed here. What better indication that this is a theory whose subject matter is that of the other theories of pleasure—that is, pleasure? Perhaps, however, I should acknowledge that there is one motivation for theories of pleasure that I have chosen not to try to make room for. That is the thought that there must be some commensurable quantity to be maximized if rational choice is always to be possible. (There may be a further thought, that our moral life would be much simpler if there were such a commensurable quantity.[31]) This thought is an expression of the conception of practical reasoning against which I am now arguing, and I do not feel that I need to be concessive toward it.

§ 6.6

Even once it has been allowed that pleasure can be understood as a kind of practical judgment, the objection may well arise that we ought not to construe these judgments as *observations*. I am going to work through a handful of variations on this objection, in order to extract what I think is the misconception of observation that motivates it, and which I will attempt to correct. Doing so will enable me to answer a question that came up at the beginning of this chapter, as to how the premises of practical inductions can differ from the instrumentalist's desires.

I have been arguing that practical reasoning can be empirical reasoning. But it will be objected that what I am claiming is empirical practical reasoning differs fundamentally from empirical theoretical reasoning, and that this is displayed in the fact that empirical theoretical reasoning converges, whereas practical empirical reasoning does not: scientists eventually agree, but policymakers don't. And scientists' theories, unlike the sides of a practical dispute, seem like approximations on the way

---

31. See Nussbaum, 1986, pp. 89–121.

to a theory that will be true once and for all.[32] The difference, it will be suggested, is this. Genuine observation is intersubjective, but pleasures are idiosyncratic: 'Chacun son goût.' 'Different strokes for different folks.' 'De gustibus non est disputandum.' Observations are observations *of* something, and if there were something being observed, people would take the same pleasures in the same things. They do not, and so the alleged observations have no objects, which is just to say that they are not observations.

This objection is a bit like an artichoke, and we are going to have to pull it apart leaf by leaf to get to the heart. (As with an artichoke, however, the leaves are part of the meal.) We can start by fielding three partial responses. First, there is somewhat more convergence in experiential judgments of desirability than the objection supposes. After all, many pleasures are sufficiently standardized to support large industries. Second, different things are desirable for different people. To the extent that pleasure covaries with these differences, variation in pleasure may be accounted for in terms of the reliability of observation.[33] Third, while there will be cases where we do not want to say that differences in desir-

---

32. Of course, these views of science have been contested, most famously by Kuhn, 1970.

33. There are analogous points to be made about the temporal variability of pleasure. Pleasure is often transient. As identical rock-bottom beliefs accumulate, conviction strengthens, but as identical 'observations' of desirability accumulate, pleasure—it will be objected—gives way to boredom. Pleasure cannot be, consequently, a proper analog of conviction.

As in the treatment of interpersonal variability in pleasure, the objection overestimates the amount of variation. Pleasures do not always become less pleasurable. Repeated wine tasting, or hiking trips, or encounters with an exotic cuisine, may make those things much more pleasurable than they were found to be at first acquaintance.

And, as before, much of the variation can be accounted for in terms of temporal variation in desirability. If I look twenty times for the milk in the refrigerator, each time I find it confirms a constant fact: that the milk is in the refrigerator throughout. But the twentieth cup of milk is not as desirable as the first; that I find it less pleasurable is a sign of the reliability of my judgment. In this, it is no different from belief: were I to make repeated observations of some changing state of affairs (say, a state of affairs that was changing *because* I was making repeated observations of it) I should find that my convictions changed with it. For example, I can request a record of my checking account's activity, for a three dollar charge. If I do this repeatedly, I shall find less and less in my account.

ability account for differences in pleasure, and where we are unwilling to correct the pleasures of either party, these are likely to be cases where the disagreement does not matter very much. Our toleration for disagreement in pleasures may be on a par with the toleration of diverging beliefs that we do not think matter very much.

Now let's suppose it conceded that differences in what is desirable for one or another person are correlated to a greater or lesser extent with differences in what is pleasurable for them. The concession will be followed by the rejoinder that the variation in desirability is to be explained by the variation in pleasure: that this is more desirable than that, for so-and-so, *because* it is more pleasurable for him. And if this is right, the rejoinder continues, pleasure cannot be observation, since observation requires the converse direction of explanation: the presence of the thing observed explains one's having the observation, and not the other way around.

This construal of the force of the objection presents it as turning on a point more formal than substantive, but the more formal claim is an inessential part of the objection, and needs to be cleared away. Even if pleasure does sometimes explain desirability, it doesn't follow that pleasure cannot be part of the cognitive process of practical observation; explanation can run in *both* directions. The rejoinder deploys an insufficiently observant notion of observation. Think of observations that are not claimed to be practical, and which contribute to the presence of what is observed: the blatancy of a contradiction has a good deal to do with how readily I notice it; the legibility, or illegibility, to me, of someone's handwriting is firmed up by my successful, or unsuccessful, attempt to read it; the lie is transparent because I (would) see through it at once. Again, the notion of social construction, popular these days in certain politicized styles of philosophy, supplies examples of communal observation constituting the facts observed: the attire is sexy because people see it that way; the comportment is masculine, or feminine, because people take it to be. And of course the words mean what they do because that is what they are heard to mean.[34]

---

34. These examples may bring secondary qualities to mind (cf. section 4.4), but I want to gesture at, rather than treat, the connections between this topic and pleasure. To

The formal difficulty, then, regarding direction of explanation, does not adequately capture the force of the objection. We can make some headway by considering a class of cases for which the objection seems clearly decisive, those in which the desirability characterization associated with the practical judgment that I claim to be, or to be part of, the experience of pleasure is given in terms of pleasure itself: that the object of pleasure is desirable precisely in that it is pleasurable. Here the problematic dependence of the desirability on the pleasure is brought to the fore in the content of the practical judgment; the twice-revised objection now points to a circularity in the content of the judgment that is incompatible with construing pleasures as observations. I'll show how this problem can be sidestepped, and then go on to say just why this circularity would be objectionable in the first place.

Consider someone who wants a piece of chocolate cake because eating it will be pleasurable. On my account, the anticipated pleasure just is the experience of finding the cake desirable; so I must say he desires the cake because he wants to find it desirable. But this is unenlightening, peculiar-sounding, and simply misses the point of the appeal to *pleasure.* Moreover, the appeal to pleasure that is causing the trouble seems hard to avoid. Suppose he believes the chocolate cake to be, all things considered, undesirable. (It is, as people say, a heart attack on a plate.) If, on the one hand, the content of the observational judgment of desirability that I am identifying with pleasure is that the cake is, all things considered, desirable, then I must take his persisting pleasure to be something like an optical illusion. This seems implausible: optical illusions are unusual, startling, and, unlike pleasure, once they are recognized, they cease to influence our judgments. On the other hand, if the content of the observational judgment is that the cake is desirable, not all things considered,

---

the extent that it is plausible that our capacities for pleasure explain the contours of desirability, they presumably do so in a way analogous to that in which our abilities to see colors, and to categorize objects as being similarly colored, explain the colors of objects. Now it is clear that in the case of colors, the paradigm case of secondary qualities, this dependence does not preclude observation. Why should it preclude observation when the observation is practical, rather than theoretical?

but in some particular respect, what is the respect in which it is desirable, if not that it is pleasurable?[35]

The way out of this problem involves a certain amount of divide-and-conquer. To begin with, we ought not to accept too quickly the claim that our man with the sweet tooth desires the cake because he wants the pleasure he gets when he eats it. Rather, what he desires are the *sensations* he will get when eating the cake, and these will be pleasurable—that is, the kind of sensations he will find to be rock-bottom desirable. Normally one does not have to distinguish feelings from the sensations they involve, but here we have no choice. Pleasure is not a sensation, and what he wants from the chocolate cake are sensations, sensations that will be desirable when he gets them.[36] And we can say either that he finds the cake desirable in respect of the sensations it produces (but not desirable, plain and simple), or that he finds the sensations plain and simple desirable.

To be sure, this method of separating desirable from undesirable aspects of an object of pleasure will not always work; perhaps an ascetic finds some sensations continuing to be pleasurable, despite being recognized as irredeemably corrupt. Cases like these I think *can* be handled on the model of persisting illusions—not, indeed, optical illusions, but what we can call *observational* illusions. I know that door-to-door vacuum cleaner salesmen are dishonest and conniving, and I also know that a trustworthy appearance is one of the tools of their devious trade; but

---

35. This objection is due to Alyssa Bernstein and Sydney Shoemaker.

36. More generally, it may be experiencing the desirable features of the cake that one is looking forward to; one need not think of oneself as a consumer of sensations.

This distinction, incidentally, makes masochism conceptually unproblematic. Masochists are people who take pleasure in pain, and the existence of such people presents a problem for philosophers who hold pain to be the converse of pleasure. (Athletes might be a less exotic case of people who can find painful sensations pleasurable.) But if the pain masochists allegedly take pleasure in is a sensation, then it is not the converse of pleasure, since pleasure is not, on my account, a sensation. What sensations are found pleasurable is not a matter of the logic of the notion of pleasure: while there may be good reasons for pain being not normally pleasurable, there is no reason in principle why sensations of pain could not engender rock-bottom judgments of desirability, that is, be pleasurable.

the vacuum cleaner salesman on my front doorstep looks trustworthy anyway. Perhaps he has such an honest face that I cannot help falling for his sales pitch, even though I know better. This would be epistemic akrasia,[37] the counterpart, in the domain of theoretical reasoning, of weakness of the will, which was traditionally described as being overcome by pleasure.

What this goes to show is that in at least a large proportion of the cases, the objectionable circularity is only apparent, and can be avoided. (I am willing to allow that there are cases in which it cannot; I suggested earlier that they can be understood on the model of the miser's attitudes toward money.) Even if it turns out that these pleasures should not be counted as successful observations, the vast majority of our pleasures do not have whatever difficulty is involved in this circularity. But what difficulty, exactly, would this be?

I take it that the problem would be this. When the content of the practical judgment we are considering is that its object is pleasurable, there is nothing, on a view that identifies the pleasure with that very judgment, to exert normative control over it. Let the object of such a practical judgment be what it may, if one has the judgment, one is correct in having it: merely having it is enough to be right about it. But if this is what is going on, then there is nothing anchoring the premises of one's practical inductions over and above one's mere reactions. Variability in pleasures is a threat to the observationalist account when it is taken to be produced by brute variation in responses. This worry needs to be addressed even once it is clear that overtly circular pleasures are unthreatening exceptions. In the vocabulary introduced in Chapter 2, pleasures of this kind involve no backward-directed inferential commitments. Now recall that the instrumentalist understanding of desire was

---

37. Hurley, 1989, pp. 130–135, 159–170, identifies the phenomenon, which she calls 'evidential akrasia', and goes on to deny that it exists. Her reason is that, "in the case of what should be believed, truth alone governs and it can't be divided against itself or harbour conflicts" (p. 133); this is supposed to license a policy of attributing to agents psychological states that avoids imputing epistemic akrasia to them. But, as we saw in section 2.4, the direct appeal to truth on the part of a would-be believer is, normally, just table-thumping. Truth is not doing any of the work; what actually does the work is one's reasons, and these can conflict.

rejected as unsatisfactory for just this reason. If pleasures do not differ from desires in this respect, they will not be the kind of thing that can make up one's mind.

To characterize a judgment as an observation is, among other things, to hold it to involve further backward-directed commitments. Which these are is exhibited in the different ways in which putative observations can be discredited: if I point out that he wouldn't recognize one if it hit him in the face, or that you're just seeing what you want to see, or that she doesn't have a very well-developed palate for these things yet, or that it's the alcohol speaking, or that they don't want to notice that they're being pandered to, I am marking backward-directed inferential commitments that the observational judgment must meet. So we can recast the objection we have been considering as follows. To call something an observation is to further imply that it will resist being discredited (in roughly the way that to call something a realization is to imply that it is true); so it might seem that for a judgment, theoretical or practical, to amount to an observation, there must be something like a *mechanism* whose operation guarantees its reliability, and accounts for its resistance to attempts to discredit it. We have seen no such mechanism, and, this version of the objection continues, there is a reason. We have on hand only the thinnest account of the object of the alleged practical observations—desirability, where this notion is admitted to be only a placeholder. Without a much more substantial account, telling us what practical observations are *of,* we will not be in a position even to investigate whether such a mechanism exists.

What is going wrong here, I think, is the idea that the explanation for an observation's not being discredited must be given in terms of something like an underlying mechanism. This idea is derived from a common philosopher's conception (or misconception) of what takes place in the course of identifying medium-sized dry goods under good light, where a familiar sketch of the perceptual mechanism is taken to underwrite the distinction between perception and illusion. But not all observation is properly understood on this model. In Almodovar's *Women on the Verge of a Nervous Breakdown* there is a character who looks like a Picasso, as though her face were one of those figures both of whose eyes are on the same side. That is an observation, but the explanation of what

makes seeing that a face looks like a Picasso an observation will have pre-
cious little in common with the explanation of what makes seeing that a
chair is brown an observation.[38] No single model of observation will do,
and we are now in a position to say why.

Novel observables require novel kinds of observation; if we were restricted to some antecedently fixed vocabulary of pleasures, the strategy
of learning what matters from experience would have few advantages
over relying on innate priorities. This explains both why we have to do
without a substantive, general account of what practical observations are
observations *of,* and why no single model of observation, mechanistic or
otherwise, will do. If there were not pliability in the means of observation corresponding to the new and different items we are going to have
to observe, our practical observations would have long since been left
behind by our changing circumstances.[39] Although Nature has equipped
us with some rock-bottom dispositions to judge this or that desirable—
say, to find food desirable after a moderately lengthy fast—pleasure depends in large part on one's tastes. Tastes, when educated, amount to
taste (if not necessarily to good taste), and taste plays much the same
role in our rock-bottom judgments of desirability that certain kinds of
background beliefs play in our acquiring rock-bottom convictions. (For
example, while I do not infer that I enjoy the painting from my knowledge of its merits, the pleasure I take in it does depend on my having that
knowledge. This is why taste can be both spontaneous and informed by
belief, discrimination, and so on.)[40] Because practical observation is what

---

38. Notice, to return to the formulation of the objection with which we began, that
there is not quite as much convergence in theoretical empirical reasoning as the objection
seems to suppose; observation is not always as intersubjective as all that. Science perhaps
converges, but not all empirical reasoning is science. I see the character's resemblance to
a Picasso, and so do some other people I have spoken to; but not everyone, even among
those familiar with Picasso, does. And I am not quite willing to insist that anyone who
does not see the resemblance is *wrong.*

39. This suggests that a long tradition of trying to make philosophical sense of perception in terms of notions like 'normal observers' and 'standard conditions' is deeply
wrongheaded. Because observation has to be able to adapt to novel circumstances, it has
to work and make sense when the observers and conditions are precisely nonstandard.

40. Explaining how this can be the case is one of the problems a theory of taste must
address. (See Schaper, 1987.) That the present account of pleasure provides means of
addressing this difficulty suggests that it may be on the right track.

enables us to learn our way around new areas of human activity, it is important that tastes can be educated.

Since I have raised the topic of taste, this is a convenient moment to return to a problem left over from the discussion of desiring at will. Remember that I deferred consideration of what looked like a way to acquire desires voluntarily, albeit indirectly: the suggestion was, it will be recalled, that one could desire 'at pill' by acquiring tastes 'at pill'.[41] We can now see that the ways in which we can acquire tastes 'at pill' must be restricted in ways reminiscent of the restrictions on acquiring desires 'at pill'. Bases for practical inferences can be discredited by showing them not to live up to the backward-directed commitments they involve, that is, when they purport to be practical observations, by showing them to be untrustworthy observations, or not to be observations at all. Under quite a wide range of circumstances, discovering that an apparently observational practical judgment is due to having taken a pill will undercut the judgment, as when my appreciation of and pleasure in the profundity of Grateful Dead lyrics is convincingly attributed to the hash brownies consumed before the concert.

I do not want to deny that *some* tastes (and so some desires) may be acquired this way, and remain stable when the manner of their acquisition is contemplated.[42] I have allowed that one's observational capacities and what one turns out to observe may vary together. But, because practical induction is important not least in that it sustains unity of agency, pills of this kind are not a way of replacing practical observation and practical induction.

The late composer John Cage is said to have had a taste for wild mushrooms, which he continued to collect and consume, despite having been hospitalized a number of times after eating the poisonous ones.

---

41. See section 2.5.

42. A taste for broccoli was suggested to me by Sydney Shoemaker as an example (1997). But the stability of even such tastes is, on second glance, perhaps more complicated a question than one might suppose. What would one think of a pill that made one prefer Kraft Processed Cheese Food Slices to a ripe Stilton, or Wonder Bread to an honest loaf? And how stable could we suppose its effects to be on someone who bothers to notice their food? (For a fascinating compendium of attentive and thoughtful practical observations on food, flavors, and eating, see Fisher, 1990, and esp. pp. 57ff; it is an interesting exercise to consider the effects of such a pill on Ms. Fisher's palate.)

Imagine inducing, with a pill, a taste like his, only perhaps slightly more extreme. Such a pill would be bound to get its user into trouble: it is not good to be extremely sick, to be put in a hospital, and to wind up at death's door, or walking through it. If experiences of this kind do not disabuse the agent of his pill-acquired taste, they are likely to make him regard his own behavior as compulsive. That is, either the pill will not work over the long run, or the user's unity of agency will be undercut.[43] (Of course, no agent is perfectly unified, and a few such tastes can perhaps be accommodated. But too many of them will not leave us with a functioning agent.)

Our practical observations are, and must be, distinguished from the instrumentalist's desires, or from mere reactions, by involving backward-directed commitments. Being able to meet these commitments is essential to maintaining unity of agency. It remains only to recast this point as an alternative to the mechanistic conception of observation.

What counts as an observation is, appropriately, an empirical matter. Observations belong to those (sometimes quite nuanced) categories of experience that we have found, empirically, can serve as observations. It is not as though we can determine, a priori, which of our practical judgments about particulars are observations, and are therefore suitable premises for inductions. (The idea that this was possible in the theoretical domain led to the myth of sense data.) Rather, in the theoretical domain as well as the practical, we determine which cat-

---

43. Developing this illustration further would recapitulate the argument of Chapter 4; I will briefly sketch the steps. Faced with the agency-eroding effects of such pills, there are evidently two ways out. We can either avoid giving agents pills that are going to get them into trouble in this way, or we can supplement their diet with still further pills meant to keep the agent's plans on track and himself unified. (For example, we can give him a pill that will make him like being extremely sick and in the hospital. It will not stop there, of course; such an attitude is bound to alienate his friends and relatives, a problem which we will want to treat with yet a further pill, one that makes him indifferent to their response. Evidently, such changes have a tendency to spread rapidly.) Either way, we will need to know which tastes are likely to get the agent into trouble of this general kind. And the only way we can usually find out about such things is practical observation and practical induction: we know that the unselective eating of wild mushrooms can make you miserable because many people have been made miserable in just this way, and we have generalized from their practical experience.

egories of judgments are observations by discovering which can *function* as observations—for instance, by figuring as premises in inductive arguments that work. The 'observations' made in dreams are not actually observations because we have found, from experience, that they can't be used that way. The observations of medium-sized dry goods under good light are observations because, we have found, they can. The backward-directed commitments involved in an observation, practical or theoretical, have to do with belonging to such a category; to impugn an observation by suggesting, for example, that so-and-so is not very discriminating, is to give reason for thinking that the dubious observation will not do the inferential work it should. (When we use the attempted observations of the undiscriminating in our practical inductions, we are let down; if we are let down too often, unity of agency starts to erode.) There is no uniform explanation of what it is to be an observation, beyond the ability to figure in inferences as an observation.

If we are on track so far, we can say what we need to about the intersubjectivity of observation very quickly. Intersubjectivity is a matter of degree, and it is entirely a matter of the inferential work a kind of observation proves able to perform. I will return to this family of issues in the next chapter.

§ 6.7

The account of pleasure that we have on the table has upshots, not only for practical induction, but for another recently popular alternative to means-end reasoning, the specification of rules or ends.[44] Deliberation consists, on the specificationist account, not, or not only, in determining what would be a means to one's already given ends, but in coming to understand what would constitute realizing a vaguely specified end, such as happiness, having an entertaining evening, a good constitution for the body politic, or a cure for an illness.[45]

---

44. Advocates include Kolnai, 1978, Wiggins, 1980, Broadie, 1987, and Richardson, 1994.

45. For these examples, see *NE* 1095a16-21, Williams, 1981a, p. 104, and Kolnai, 1978, pp. 44f. The example of happiness, or *eudaemonia,* is a favorite, and on this point

Now while it is clear enough that we do engage in mental activity of this kind, it may be less clear that this activity is subject to the normative constraints that would allow us to regard it as reasoning or as deliberation, properly so-called. In fact, two prominent expositors of the specificationist view deny that specification of ends is a legitimate form of reasoning. Kolnai describes it as "shot through with arbitrariness", and "an inherently deceptive, not to say deceitful operation";[46] and Broadie, in a passage that perhaps clarifies Kolnai's qualms about the specification of ends, presents an argument to the effect that such specification cannot be "inferential": because the specification of an end

> is a move from the less to the more determinate, which latter, precisely because it is more determinate, cannot be entailed by what is less so. It might seem that with suitable extra premises there could be a logically acceptable inference from the indeterminate to the determinate end. After all, there is no acceptable inference from the determinate end to the means except via additional [empirical] premisses . . . But . . . what additional premises would do the trick? (a) Factual ones, whether particular or general, would not help; nor (b) would any purely logical propositions. The addition (c) of some formal propositions about *eupraxia* [the end whose specification Broadie is discussing], such as that it is 'self-sufficient' or 'lacking in nothing,' would not logically enable one to interpret the pursuit of *eupraxia* as the pursuit of S (where S is

---

I have to part ways with what seem to be the majority of specificationists. I am inclined to think that the function of happiness in practical reasoning is not that of a goal, but, rather, resembles what Kant called regulative ideals. One must act on the assumption that it is possible to arrange one's central (and, maybe, not-so-central) goals into a coherent and (in principle) satisfiable goal or life-plan: taken together, the things one (really) wants make up a picture of a life well-lived. This may not in fact be the case; having to act as though one's ends allow this does not entail that they actually do. (Kant distinguished regulative ideals from the necessary preconditions of the possibility of experience.)

Kant thought, it seems to me correctly, that we are unable to determine what happiness would consist in early on enough for it to be a starting point for means-end reasoning; only much later, if ever, can we see what contribution our choices have made to our happiness. (Cf. note 19, section 3.5.) If this is right, then the progress that we do make in arriving at a conception of happiness has a far more oblique relation to choice than some specificationists assume.

46. Kolnai, 1978, pp. 54, 58.

something more specific); whereas (d) inserting a premiss that specifies *eupraxia* substantially might of course sustain the inference to a no less substantial conclusion, but only by thrusting back to an earlier stage the problem of how such propositions are obtained in the first place.[47]

Suppose I am faced with the problem mentioned by Williams, that of deciding what would make for an entertaining evening. Mummenschanz is at the McCarter Theater, and I have not seen them, nor, I gather, anything like them, before. I have factual premises, in the form of a friend's description ("they mime inanimate objects"), and these premises do not help. Logical and formal propositions do not help either. What I need is a premise of Broadie's type (d), one that specifies my end of being entertained substantially and in the relevant respects: I need to know whether Mummenschanz will *count as* entertainment, that is, whether it will *be* entertaining.

As Broadie insists, the demand for such premises raises "the problem of how such propositions are obtained in the first place". She evidently

---

47. Broadie, 1987, pp. 238f. Her argument involves a problematic premise: that the more determinate cannot be inferentially extracted from the less. After all, if the determinateness of one's starting point is not *stipulatively* linked to the determinateness of one's conclusion, we may expect to find any number of counterexamples in which determinateness increases as the inference is traversed. (Turning over several indistinct and obscure recollections of the previous day, I suddenly realize *exactly* what Sandra is up to.)

But the implausible premise may be defended. Broadie's argument is intended to show that specification of ends is not an alternative to means-end reasoning. Now it is an unfortunate feature of the manner in which this putative alternative is discussed that it is not always made clear that there are two ways in which ends can be specified, and that one of these *is* means-end reasoning. When I ascertain that only one quite precisely specified action satisfies a number of perhaps rather vaguely given constraints, as when I find that only one movie is close enough, inexpensive enough, and sufficiently promising to lay claim to my evening, I may be said to have moved inferentially from the less to the more determinate; however, my reasoning has been entirely instrumental. But Broadie presumably wishes to exclude this type of reasoning from the scope of her argument. If specification of ends can legitimately proceed from the less to the more determinate only when it is joint constraint satisfaction, and if (an equally large 'if') reasoning about how to jointly satisfy constraints is instrumental reasoning, then it is not implausible that specification of ends that is not means-end reasoning—that is, the kind of specification in which Broadie is interested—will not be able legitimately to move from less determinate premises to more determinate conclusions.

intends mention of the problem to have the force of a rhetorical question, since she concludes that no such premises are available. But consideration of a concrete situation in which the demand arises makes it obvious how such premises *are* obtained: I can *go* to McCarter, and discover, by observation, whether Mummenschanz is entertaining or not. That is, specification of ends can be understood to be a form of rational deliberation, but one that, like the practical analog of induction, relies essentially on practical experience.[48] If this is right, then there is more than one kind of empirical practical reasoning.

The example reminds us that actual judgments of desirability, experiential or otherwise, are normally a good deal richer than those to which I have, for expository convenience, largely confined myself. To attend the performance and thereby discover that Mummenschanz is vastly entertaining is of course to discover that attending the performance is in certain respects desirable, and it is to have taken a good deal of pleasure in the performance, but my response, and what I have found out, is not exhausted by these descriptions: pleasure typically makes its appearance as a facet of any of a wide range of emotional responses. (Think of the pleasure involved in relief, for example.) I suggested in the introduction that an account of practical reasoning has upshots for the philosophy of mind, and we have, in Chapter 2, already seen one of these: belief-desire psychology is a mistake, its desires infrequent and unimportant, and 'direction of fit' an unhelpful way of distinguishing between and understanding mental states. Our discussion of the role of pleasure in practical reasoning, and the continuity that I have just gestured at, between pleasure and other emotions, suggests that feelings, by contrast, are very important. The emotions are difficult terrain for philosophers of mind, and understanding them has rarely been regarded as urgent. But if our discussion is on track, we can no longer afford to leave them on the back burner. The emotions deserve philosophical attention they have not been getting.

---

48. Testimony may of course take the place of experience, as when I am told not only that the performance is mime of such-and-such a kind, but that it is vastly entertaining. But here I rely on experience indirectly. I will consider testimony further in the next chapter.

§ 6.8

There are two subject matters, not always clearly distinguished, that philosophers usually have in mind when they use words like 'ethics' or 'morals'.[49] One is, roughly, the art and science of being nice to people you don't like, and while I don't have anything against being nice, I'm going to leave this area of expertise to one side for the moment. The other is, again roughly, the science of what people ought to be doing. On this latter conception of ethics, a successful moral or ethical theory would be a general and systematic characterization of what actions should be performed, what decisions made, and what policies undertaken. But this is to say that an ethical theory should be related to practical reasoning as product to process: after all, practical reasoning just is figuring out what the right actions, decisions and policies are.

I have been arguing that practical reasoning is *empirical.* Much practical reasoning is inductive, that is, it arrives at more general practical judgments by generalizing from more particular ones; and these particular practical judgments are largely—directly or indirectly—the deliverances of experience. One's conclusions as to what to do are as responsible to experience as one's conclusions about what to believe.

If practical reasoning is empirical, then ethical theory should be empirical too. If one's ethical theory, that is, one's systematic and general theory about what to do, is arrived at in large part through practical induction, then it is beholden to, and should be tested against, ethical experience. The reader familiar with contemporary moral philosophy will recognize that this view is very much at odds with the way ethical theorizing is carried on these days. Armchair theories are the rule; these are produced through a peculiar ritual in which one is asked to imagine some set of circumstances, and is then invited to have an 'intuition'— a moral reaction to the imagined situation. Moral theories are treated as supported or impugned by the agreement or disagreement of 'intuition' with their pronouncements.

---

49. Some philosophers distinguish ethics from morals; here I'm going to treat the terms as near-synonyms.

I don't mean to deny that thought experiments in ethics can be valuable. (Thought experiments are valuable in the acknowledgedly empirical natural sciences.) But the claims of a moral theory need to be tested against observations, not just against 'intuitions', and not just through imaginative exercises. There is all the difference in the world between *imagining* what would happen and what it would be like, and *seeing* what *does* happen and what it *is* like. You would not expect to learn how the battle is going to turn out, or what you will find exploring a foreign city, or whether you have left the keys in the car, or whether matter is made of indivisible atoms, by *imagining* the battle, the city, and so on. Why would anyone have ever thought that you could learn whether battles are glorious or shameful, whether exploring a foreign city will be wonderful or tedious, whether forgetting the car keys would be reprehensible, or which of the right and the good is prior to the other, through *imagination*?

If the inductive account of practical reasoning is correct, the method of much contemporary moral theorizing has very little to be said for it. But when the method is flawed, we should expect the conclusions to be untrustworthy. It is quite likely that some 'intuitions' inadvertently incorporate lessons learned from experience, but where there is nothing like systematic and self-conscious responsibility to observation, we have no reason to think that an 'intuition'-based moral theory is going to be any better than the fantastic constructions of an armchair scientist. If ethics is an empirical science, and if the ethical theories that today hold the field are the product not of empirical investigation, but of 'intuition'-based methods, then we have very little inducement to think those theories satisfactory.[50]

---

50. For further discussion of the consequences of theories of practical reasoning for moral philosophy, see Millgram, 1997b.

7

How to Win Friends and Influence People

The analogies between theoretical and practical reasoning which we have encountered so far suggest that, just as the premises of theoretical inductions come not only from one's own observations, but from others' testimony, so practical inductions can be expected to derive some of their premises from a practical analog of testimony. And this needs only to be said in order to be acknowledged as true: of course we (sometimes) take advice, accept others' practical judgments of the worth or necessity of doing this or that, and trust what people tell us about what we really want. Still, one might think that practical testimony was merely a shortcut, dispensable in principle, to results obtainable by practical observation: what you learn from others, you could have found out by going and seeing for yourself. So I will first argue that practical testimony is not dispensable. Then I will characterize more concretely the notion of reliance that is required by the argument; it will prove to be broader in some respects, and narrower in others, than that of practical testimony, and will have the surprising upshot that another person's mental states can be, literally, one's own. It will also serve as the basis for a partial account of love or friendship; if this account is on the right track, then the latter subject is far more closely connected to foundational issues in ethics and in epistemology than is normally supposed.

§ 7.1

Why isn't testimony dispensable? Is there a principled reason why an extremely cautious agent couldn't make inferences only from theoretical or practical judgments acquired in the course of his own observations, and yet still have a rich and accurate understanding of his world, and a satisfactory system of ends and practical judgments related to them? Even if the way in which human beings grow and develop psychologically precludes actually acquiring one's take on things in this way, mightn't it in principle be possible, proceeding in the spirit of Carnap or Reichenbach, to rationally reconstruct one's body of knowledge or practical judgments, in a way that gives no independent authority to reliance on testimony?

Consider first traditional, theoretical induction. Induction is defeasible: the inference from 'Raven *A* is black', 'Raven *B* is black', 'Raven *C* is black', and 'Raven *D* is black', to 'All ravens are black' is defeated by 'Ravens *A*, *B*, *C*, and *D* are freshly painted'. One has not mastered the technique of inductive inference if one's inductive inferences are not sensitive to such defeating conditions. But notice what is required for such sensitivity. For one thing, it depends on background beliefs, to the effect that painting something can change its color, that the color of an animal generally does not covary with the colors of other animals of that species unless it is that animal's natural color, and so on. (If birds' coloring were a matter of avian fashion, painting a few ravens might start a black plumage craze, and in that case, the induction would, perhaps, not be defeated by the ravens' having been recently painted.) That means that mastery of the technique of inductive inference requires having available a pool of background beliefs.

Where do the background beliefs required for an induction come from? As the example suggests, they are bound to include somewhat general, if also domain-specific, facts, and since only particulars are observed, this means that they cannot be entirely a matter of observation. Perhaps some of these general beliefs are in turn the products of induction; in that case we can ask where the background beliefs required for those inductions are from. If we follow such a chain of inductions back, we will eventually come to an initial induction, perhaps a toddler's awkward first generalization.[1] But this induction, too, requires a background pool of relevant and general beliefs; these, by hypothesis, cannot have been inductively arrived at. Where are they from?

If the agent's earliest inductions date to his very early childhood, then we know where they are from: they are beliefs he has acquired from his parents (or other people in his environment). These beliefs are simply taken on faith. The very small child is not in a position to assess inductively the reliability of the opinions his parents convey to him; until he has a supply of such opinions, he is not yet equipped to engage in inductive inference. This need for an initial stock of reliable beliefs about a domain is not just a feature of actual human psychological development; attempts at rational reconstruction that face up to the defeasibility of basic patterns of inference will also require, at the outset of the reconstruction, a supply of general beliefs that cannot themselves have been inductively arrived at.

It might be objected here that a regress of this kind cannot just terminate in one's parents' opinions; after all, where did those opinions come from? Must it not have been possible, at what for that very reason would have turned out to be the dawn of human history, to have arrived at more or less reliable beliefs through inductions that did not presuppose further, inherited beliefs? The objection points up an important feature of the argument, that it relies on an apparently contingent fact about human beings: roughly, that we are not born with a sufficiently large supply of innate beliefs that could, by themselves, get inductions off the ground. (While human individuals are not, evidently the human species as a whole is; evolutionary pressures must have mimicked the presence of the requisite innate beliefs.)

Is it simply an accident of human nature that we lack the innate beliefs that would make this kind of early reliance on others unnecessary? Not quite; we can better see the advantages of coming by our initial beliefs this way if we consider an area in which we are built—hard-wired—to come to have somewhat general judgments triggered by,

---

1. Of course, actual human development is not as straightforward as this; just as infants only gradually come to walk, so their mental operations only gradually resolve themselves into inferences. For present purposes, these complications can be set aside.

but not inductively inferred from, observations. On current accounts of language learning, human beings acquire the grammar of their mother tongue not by inductively constructing a theory that accounts for the evidence of their ears, but through a process in which minimal exposure to the language generates rules of grammar, as it were by toggling switches in a template. Without this hard-wired shortcut, a small child would be unable to understand what its parents tell it; evidently, our ability to use testimony depends on having some such built-in capacity.

There might be—we might have been—creatures who were built to acquire their initial induction-enabling stock of generalizations in more or less the way we acquire our mother tongues. Such creatures perhaps would not need to rely on testimony. They would, however, have to count on artificially stable environments in which to do their initial learning; only if one's initial generalizations are more or less on target will they contribute to the sensitivities needed for practical induction, and generalizations produced reflexively will, barring exceptional good luck, be on target only when the environment and the reflexes are tailored to one another. Human beings can learn the grammar of their mother tongue in this way only because grammars are constrained in ways that make them learnable.

So although there are very limited areas in which we can come up to speed using innate belief, or something tantamount to it, rather than testimony, we are not built this way through and through, and there is a reason we are not. We need induction in the first place because we need to be able to learn from experience, and we need to be able to learn from experience because novelty is so pervasive. There are indefinitely many domains in which we may need to make inductions, and new ones come along all the time. When it's not possible to anticipate what domains a creature will be required to make its initial inductions in, or what those domains will be like, it's not possible to construct a creature to see the general facts about these domains that would underwrite inductions in them. (It makes no difference to this point whether we are considering inscribing the facts as innate knowledge on the infant's nascent mind, or having the relevant judgments triggered by observation of particulars.) If one is to design a creature to cope with novelty, it makes far more sense to specify, as part of the design, that it will have informants able to tell it what it needs to know to get started, and then equip it to take advantage of that fact by relying on them. It would be too much to ask of evolution, or even of God, to have infants be able to pick up the traffic laws on their own, and to realize that they had better not cross against the light. After all, when people were being designed (or being 'designed'), there were neither traffic laws nor traffic lights. Much better to have parents learn about traffic lights, and children able to listen to their parents.

§ 7.2

What goes for theoretical induction goes, in this case, for practical induction also. Practical induction is a defeasible pattern of inference; and, as its theoretical analog suggests, the sensitivity to defeating conditions that is necessary for mastery of this very basic form of practical inference requires the availability of further practical judgments, among these, somewhat general practical judgments. My inference from 'Drink *A* was a good idea', 'Drink *B* was a good idea', and 'Drink *C* was a good idea', to 'Further drinks would be a good idea' is defeated by (among other things) my having to drive home later on; that in turn requires that I understand, even if imperfectly, the importance both of my own life and of the lives of the anonymous others I may encounter on the road.

As we saw in Chapter 3, practical inductions are not the only form of practical inference that requires a stock of somewhat general practical judgments in the background. The argument of that chapter turned on the fact that practical syllogisms are another pattern of defeasible inference. It is part of being able to reason with practical syllogisms that one have at least a rough and ready understanding of when *not* to draw the syllogism's conclusion—that is, of what the syllogism may be defeated by. For example, the premises 'Eat delicious things' and 'This cake is delicious' may be used to draw the conclusion 'Eat this cake'; but the inference is non-deductive, and can be defeated by such facts as the cake's being poisoned. Someone who does not exhibit awareness of this kind of defeasibility is simply incapable of deploying the mode of practical inference we represent as the practical syllogism; he lacks mastery of a piece of essential logical apparatus. As it happens, the background practical judgments that this inference requires the agent to have at his fingertips are very close to those of the previous example: the agent needs to understand that it is important not to die.

Where do these further practical judgments come from? As before, some are perhaps derived from observation, but, because observation can only supply particular rather than general judgments, and because the background judgments must include general judgments, observation cannot supply them all. Many are certainly arrived at via practical inductions; but those inductions in turn require a further pool of practical judgments to support their own defeasibility conditions. Once again, if we follow a chain of practical inductions back to its starting point, we will find a supply of somewhat general practical judgments that are not themselves inductively arrived at. And when we ask where these come from, we will find the young child taking them on trust from, normally, his parents.[2]

Of course, although I have been emphasizing the trust that allows the very small child to bootstrap his defeasible inferential (and observational) processes, it is not as though the kind of trust I am considering is confined to early childhood. It is clear enough that adults also rely on the practical judgments of others. Trust in later life is just as much a starting point and basis of practical inference as it is early on. And if, as I am about to argue, it is rational to trust the practical judgments of others at the outset, there is a parity argument at hand in favor of trusting as an adult if one is rational to trust as an infant: if one ought to treat initial testimony as reliable, why not subsequent testimony?[3]

It is in any case not as though one could somehow reduce the force of subsequent testimony to that of initial testimony and induction. Let's distinguish two kinds of trust in testimony: reducible and primitive. Perhaps some trust in testimony is reducible. I have watched my underling

---

2. For a realistic description of these practical judgments and the way in which they are conveyed, see Barry, 1990, pp. 55f.

3. Appeals to parity need to be cashed out by showing that the same kinds of consideration are at work in both cases. I have been confining the discussion to the relatively crisp case of an agent starting entirely from scratch; one could construct a parallel and slightly messier argument for the adult case by examining an agent's first practical inductions in an entirely novel domain.

quite carefully for some time, and established, inductively, that most of what he says, in our shared area of expertise, is reliable: I can, I decide, trust his judgment, both theoretical and practical. But much trust is, by contrast, primitive. Where I am not myself an expert, I am not in a position to ascertain another's expertise on my own. It is not as though I have scrutinized my neighbors and interlocutors with the kind of thoroughness that would be needed to establish reliability in this way. Who can honestly say that he could provide *arguments,* of the kind I was prepared to produce regarding my underling—that is, the arguments required to effect a rational reconstruction of one's system of judgments that accords no independent authority to testimony—in any but a small minority of those cases in which he trusts the (practical or theoretical) judgments of others?[4] Reducible trust is rare, and so primitive trust in testimony is in-

---

4. For some discussion of related issues, see Coady, 1992. Hardwig, 1985, argues that the scale and cooperative nature of science require scientists to rely on each others' results. Ross, 1986, and Austin, 1979, esp. pp. 82, 99ff, 114f, argue for trust from the requirements of our communicative practices. Welbourne, 1986, is specifically an analysis of knowledge. See also Anscombe, 1981, Baier, 1986, Fleischacker, 1994, ch. 4, McDowell, 1980, and Shoemaker, 1963, ch. 6, esp. pp. 247–254.

Gibbard, 1990, has recently argued for relying on the judgments of others, and although he backs off when it comes to practical or normative judgments (pp. 276f), I think this is a mistake on his part: if his arguments work at all, they work here too. This makes his discussion close enough to mine for distinguishing them to be worthwhile. Gibbard's arguments have two components: parity and cost. I have relied on others' judgments in the past, and relying on them in the future is like having relied on them in the past; I grant authority to my own past judgments, and my past self is like another person, so why should I not grant authority to the judgments of others (178f)? And I cannot stop relying on my own past judgments, or the judgments of others that I have accepted in the past: that would be "to settle for a kind of hyperskepticism" (178), or to be forced "to correct my thinking beyond all recognition . . . If I could reject wholesale the past fundamental influence of others, it would carry a prohibitive cost" (179). There is a secondary argument, to the effect that not accepting the authority of others would prevent consensus from emerging: Once again, "[t]he price explains why fundamental disagreement should be so disturbing a prospect" (198).

Appealing to cost considerations seems to require justification; Gibbard makes a surprisingly similar case for cost considerations being 'granted sway': "We have all in fact been influenced by pragmatic considerations, and influenced deeply, if my evolutionary speculation is on track. If such influences do not make for good normative judgment, we are hopeless as normative judges" (226). "If we were to reject all such influence as distorting, we would have to reject all our normative judgments as products of distorting

evitably pervasive, not only among the very young, but among those we regard as mature adults. As we will see shortly, the adult case is of great philosophical interest.

§ 7.3

I will now argue that testimony is a legitimate and acceptable source of practical judgments. (I will confine myself here to primitive trust in testimony; reducible trust is a derivative, and less interesting, case.) Because the pieces of the argument are already in place, and because the style of argument is already familiar, we can be expeditious. Within the context of first-person practical deliberation, we are authorized to suppose that we are unified agents, and we are accordingly authorized to suppose that the preconditions of unified agency are satisfied; in Chapters 3 and 4 I argued that the usability of practical induction was among those preconditions. Now we have just seen that practical inductions presuppose the availability of a pool of practical judgments acquired by accepting others' testimony on trust. One's practical induc-

---

influences . . . [T]his . . . is . . . a pragmatic argument against antipragmatic purism" (223). In other words, the costs of not taking costs into account are just too high.

Where Gibbard's arguments turn on the costs of rejecting sources of authority, mine turn on what must be presupposed if one is engaged in a particular cognitive project. His view, that we should accept sources of authority because of the costs of rejecting them, fits very poorly with the arguments developed in Chapter 2: one cannot, without self-deception, believe or desire something just because not doing so carries penalties, and I do not see that distinguishing between "treating pragmatic considerations as evidence directly" and "granting them sway" (224) affects the point. In short, although the conclusions of our arguments converge, Gibbard's arguments and my own work very differently.

It is worth remarking that Gibbard's arguments face a difficulty that mine do not: the argument he uses to justify appealing to cost considerations is circular. Gibbard acknowledges this, responding that "[t]he pragmatic stakes, though, turn out to be great" (223). We are asked to "absorb the influence of this pragmatic consideration . . . [and] judge that antipragmatic purism is unreasonable" (224). But appeal to the magnitude of a consideration is irrelevant if that consideration is illegitimate in the first place. Consider an analogously constructed argument, perhaps an *ad hominem* argument in favor of *ad hominem* arguments: I claim that my opponent, who does not believe in *ad hominem* arguments, is a bad man. It is no response to the objection of circularity to insist that my opponent is not just bad, but very, very, very bad.

tions are legitimate only if such trust is; if it is misplaced, our practical inductions will go bizarrely haywire. And so, one is warranted in supposing, within the context of practical deliberation, that such trust *is* legitimate.

We can retrace the last few steps at a somewhat higher resolution by invoking once again the notions introduced in Chapter 2. Our inductions are satisfactory only if our grasp of their defeasibility conditions is. This means that among the backward-directed inferential commitments assumed in the course of a practical induction are commitments regarding the practical judgments whose presence makes possible the necessary sensitivity to the induction's defeasibility conditions. (For example, I take seriously the practical induction that tells me that I should take another trip to Mendocino, in part because I can count on being sensitive to reasons not to draw that conclusion; and that in turn means taking seriously the practical judgments that would underwrite those reasons.) If we follow the chains of backward-directed commitments to their starting-points, we find practical testimony, taken on trust. So my practical inductions, whose efficacy I must presuppose, involve commitments to the efficacy of taking practical testimony on trust. When I am engaged in practical deliberation, I must act on the assumption that primitive testimony is a rationally acceptable source of practical judgments.[5]

Showing that one must be willing to rely on primitive practical testimony does not mean that trust must be blind. The practical judgments that we assume from our parents and friends are as defeasible as any other practical judgments. Our reliance on what others tell us itself involves further backward-directed inferential commitments; when we find that these cannot be met, our trust in that source of testimony quite properly fades. (Even trust is defeasible—or rather, trust is *especially* defeasible.) I follow the recommendations of my elder and better, but not after I no-

---

5. The argument survives even when adjusting one's system of practical judgments in the direction of greater coherence is taken to be a legitimate form of practical inference. I can only put stock in the adjusted system of judgments if it was reasonable to put stock in its predecessor, and so the regress argument requires that one be able to put stock in the one's initial, testimony-derived system of practical judgments.

tice that they work out badly; I take my cue from a well-known critic only until I realize that his taste is not to be relied upon; I am deeply perturbed by my friend's criticism of my character until I see the ways in which it is self-serving. Trust is rational only because we are willing to retract it when it is broken, or abused, or proven to be otherwise misplaced.

Small children might seem to be an exception to this last claim, since one might think that the trust children place in their parents is necessarily blind. But children grow up, and when they do, they are able to critically reassess and to reject practical testimony they had earlier accepted. (This process is a rather prominent part of adolescence; and even small children will thumb their noses at their parents from behind their backs.)[6] Rejecting the trustworthiness of all testimony is cutting off the branch on which one is perched, but any particular piece of testimony can be rejected.

The argument I have just given shows that we must take primitive testimony to be a legitimate source of practical judgments. But it does not show that testimony is guaranteed to be reliable, any more than the argument on which it rests shows that practical induction is guaranteed to work. (However, because of the role played by unity of agency in the argument, it is possible to argue that having been raised on generally unreliable practical testimony would have undercut one's unity of agency. This implies that if one is lucky enough to be a reasonably unified agent, that in itself is good evidence that one's upbringing has bequeathed one practical testimony that was reliable *enough*.) And just as the earlier argument for the legitimacy of practical inductions did not provide a way of telling which practical inductions are legitimate, so this argument does not provide a way of telling which practical testimony to trust. Finally for now, a remark on the role of practical observation is in place. It is quite often the possibility of practical observation that makes it possible to suppose that the backward-directed inferential commitments involved in trusting the practical testimony of others can be met; we may accept another's advice because we are willing to believe that his experience backs it up. But, as the argument shows, this doesn't mean that practical

---

6. I'm grateful to Stanley Cavell for bringing this last point to my attention.

testimony is dispensable in favor of practical observation. Perhaps what one is being told is something one could go and see for oneself. But even if it were true of each item of testimony one rationally accepts, that one might have learned it oneself, it would not follow that one could have learned all of it via one's own experience. Starting from scratch is not an option.

§ 7.4

The argument so far has been quite abstract, and it is time to supplement it with a more substantive depiction of primitive reliance on practical testimony. Doing this is also an opportunity to address, in something of a backhanded manner, one of the problems remarked upon at the end of the previous section. The conclusion that we need to trust others' practical testimony does not tell us whom to trust; obviously, we do not trust just anybody. In the following sections, I will argue that we trust our friends. I will also try to show that an account of practical testimony provides the elements of a philosophical account of love or friendship.

A preliminary remark or two is in order. First, I will be using the words 'love' and 'friendship' as though they were translations of the Greek *philia*—that is, as applying primarily to relations between and feelings typically directed toward close relatives and companions, but not to specifically erotic or sexual relations and emotions. Second, I won't try to show that all friendship involves trust of the kind with which I am concerned, and the claims that I make about friendship at the out-set of the argument should accordingly be taken as illustrative; they are intended to help the reader identify a familiar phenomenon, and not as a way of insisting that the form of friendship in which this phe-nomenon is prominent is the only kind of friendship there is. And third, the reader should be warned that the claim that one trusts one's friends will need further elucidation once more of the supporting argument is in place.

Friends play a large role in the evolution and alteration of our systems of practical judgments. We have all been introduced to new pursuits by friends, been forced to rethink our convictions when friends have questioned our moral judgment, and have had to revise our self-images in response to critical appraisals on the part of those we love. And, of course, the development of a friendship is itself a matter of the revision of one's system of practical judgments, in that one acquires the ends involved in the friendship: one comes to desire the welfare of the friend, the friend's company, and so on. One tends to take a friend's practical judgments more seriously than those of a relative stranger, at least about some things: a close friend's judgment that, for instance, one has been insensitive is much more likely to prompt soul-searching and the consequent revision of one's attitudes than will the same judgment rendered by someone who is not a friend.

What reasons do we have for taking a friend's ethical or practical views seriously? For one thing, usually our friends know us well, and we know them well enough to trust their judgment—or to know how far we can trust it. (It is often the case that we befriend those whose systems of practical judgments are similar to our own, and so we are able to count on, e.g., their ethical views being fairly close to ours.) When this kind of reason is in play, relying on a friend can be underwritten by inductive argument.

But friends can exert a much more direct influence on one's system of practical judgments than this. It's worth recalling at this point Aristotle's thoughtful discussion of friendship, and his repeated description of the friend as another self.[7] This suggestive locution advises us to approach the topic of friendship by considering what it is to be one's *own* self. Now a particularly basic and prominent feature of being one's own self is the relation one stands in to one's own mental or cognitive states, in particular, to one's theoretical and practical judgments. The particular feature I have in mind is perhaps best exhibited by contrasting it with the relation one has to *another's* mental states or judgments.

One's own beliefs, desires, ends, pleasures, and practical judgments of other kinds enter into one's thinking *directly*, that is, as a basis for inference. For example, if I believe that *p*, I am willing to infer things from *p*. But if I discover that Smith believes that *p*, no such inferences are directly underwritten. (They may be *indirectly* underwritten. For

---

7. *NE* viii–ix; for discussion of Aristotle's views on *philia,* see Millgram, 1987.

example, if I believe that Smith is an expert in his field, then if p is in his area of expertise, his belief that p may be *evidence* that p. But my own inferences that proceed from my belief that p generally do not take this path; I do not take my beliefs that p to be *evidence* that p. Rather, my inferences proceed directly from p.) If I want X, I may begin calculating straight off how to get X. That is, if I have a goal, I take the fact that bringing about such-and-such would be a way of attaining the goal to be prima facie reason to bring about such-and-such; whereas if *Smith* has a goal, the correlative fact will seem to me to be no (direct) reason at all. (Again, it can be an *indirect* reason; if Smith is a client of mine, I may have a further interest in realizing his goals.) If I find that Smith and I have incompatible goals, this need be no occasion for examination and revision of my desires; indeed, it may even prompt me to consider how I may thwart his desires to the advantage of my own. However, if I find that I have incompatible desires, this may be an occasion for revising them. (I'll return to this topic below.) And, whether or not one accepts the account of pleasure developed in the last chapter, my own pleasures have a very different (and far more intimate) relation to my motivations than Smith's pleasures. In short, a mental state or attitude's being *mine* is in large part a matter of its being a possible basis for inference. I will say that the relation one has toward one's own attitudes or mental states is *inferentially direct*.

This contrast is crisp, however, only provided that Smith is not a friend of mine. For if Smith *were* a friend, then my relation to many of his practical judgments *would* be inferentially direct. To make things less confusing, let's contrast Smith, a stranger, with Jones, my close friend. If Jones is my friend, the fact that Jones wants p is often a direct (if not necessarily overriding) reason to bring about p.[8] The fact that he takes pleasure in such-and-such has immediate consequences for my motivations in much the way that the fact that I take pleasure in such-and-such

---

8. That is: if Jones wants to eat a piece of cake, that isn't a reason for *me* to eat a piece of cake; rather, it is a reason for me to, say, cut him a slice. A related point, brought to my attention by Hilary Putnam, is that there are things that my friend must do for himself; I cannot do them for him. This does not impugn the inferential directness of my relation to my friend's ends, however: I have, at any rate, reason to get out of his way.

does. For example, the fact that Jones would enjoy a subscription to *Philosophical Anecdotes* is a reason to get it for him when his birthday rolls around. No *further* intermediate reasons are needed. And one may even stand in inferentially direct relations to certain of the friend's beliefs, those within what Aristotle regards as the domain of *homonoia,* the shared views typical of friendship;[9] I'll consider such cases further below.

This is quite a varied collection of attitudes, but recall that the notion of a practical judgment is a catch-all placeholder for whatever the attitudes that figure in practical reasoning turn out to be. To stand in an inferentially direct relation to another's practical judgment is to exhibit primitive trust in it. And since standing in an inferentially direct relation to another's practical judgment is not to have direct epistemic access to it—inferentially direct relations are not a form of telepathy—it is to trust another's testimony, or an expression of his attitude that for present purposes can be considered to be of a piece with testimony.

I am now going to argue that inferentially direct relations to others' attitudes can be used to reconstruct a number of the familiar features of friendship. And, on the way, I will also show that an account of friendship that appeals to inferentially direct relations does better on these counts than its nearest competitors.

§ 7.5

It might be agreed that one prominent characteristic of friendship is a willingness to accommodate one's friend's desires (willingness to accommodate his pleasures being treated as a special case of this). But it might be suggested that this is not a matter of standing in inferentially direct relations to them; rather, it is simply that friendship constitutively involves having a standing desire that his desires be satisfied.[10] However, there are two reasons not to adopt this way of thinking about the matter. First, while one *can* ascribe to oneself a desire of this kind, in many cases such ascriptions do no explanatory work; and when they do not, they tend to be misleading. What more reason do I have for ascribing to myself such a desire directed toward my friend than one directed toward

---

9. *NE* 1167a22–b15.
10. This objection is due to Brian Loar.

myself? That is, if I am to account for my responsiveness to *his* desires by positing a background desire that they be satisfied, why must I not account for my responsiveness to *my* desires by positing a background desire that *my* desires be satisfied? But it is clear enough that in my own case such a desire can explain nothing: if my responsiveness to my own desires is not intelligible on its own, invoking a further desire, one to which I must be responsive if it is to serve any explanatory function, will not help. Why suppose that more explanation is needed when the desire is my friend's rather than my own?[11]

The second reason for not appealing to a background desire of this kind is that there are further phenomena that are, on the one hand, of a piece with my relation to my friend's desires, but, on the other, not even superficially amenable to this kind of construal. I will discuss two of these now.[12]

There is a class of reasons that often play a role in non-instrumental justifications; these are reasons for an end that are intelligible *as* reasons only when one already has the end. I will call such reasons *end-intrinsic.* Some examples: I can see what the point of playing the game is only once I *am* playing (or, more precisely, once I have learned to play the game,

---

11. For the classic discussion of the explanatory roles played by ascriptions of desire, see Nagel, 1978.

It might be thought that there is still a substantive difference between the two cases. When I state 'I desire that p', I am expressing a motivation, or perhaps a judgment of desirability; when I state 'He desires that p', I am stating a psychological fact—or so it might be claimed. (Compare: 'I believe that p' is a way of asserting p with reservations; 'He believes that p' states a fact about him but takes no stand whatsoever on p.) The problem with this objection is that it assumes that we have a grip on the content of an utterance that is independent of its inferential role. If my relation to his attitudes is inferentially direct, then 'He desires that p' will be an expression of motivation, or a judgment of desirability, just as 'I desire that p' is. (If I have a guru, I may use 'He believes that p' as a way of asserting p.)

12. Others deserve mention, although I cannot here consider them at length. First, empathy, that is, feeling one's friend's emotions, is a central part of *philia;* and it is not plausibly made sense of in terms of standing background desires. Second, I have suggested that one stands in inferentially direct relations to certain of one's friend's beliefs; but beliefs, as we noted in Chapter 2, are generally not explicable by appeal to second-order desires. (The most prominent relevant exception, it will be recalled, is self-deception; it would be unfortunate, however, to end up having to suppose that self-deception is a central feature of friendship.)

which, let us suppose, requires having actually played it). But to be *playing* the game, rather than merely going through the motions, I have to have adopted its goals (which may be scoring points, or more delicate matters having to do with gracefulness and sportsmanship) as my own. Asked why I am friends with so-and-so, I may adduce the great times we have together; but these great times are great *qua* time well-spent with my friend. (Of course, I may enjoy my friend's company in ways that I could enjoy a stranger's as well; but it is a central feature of friendship that I do not enjoy it in *only* those ways.) And the practice of philosophy itself is riddled with end-intrinsic reasons, which is perhaps one of the main obstacles to teaching it. If one lacks appreciation for a certain discipline-specific fluency and incisiveness of argument, or for the type of illuminating example that can seem to be the philosopher's stock-in-trade, or for the way in which philosophical argument so often moves backward, to premises and their presuppositions, rather than forward, toward (thinks the novice) constructive conclusions, then philosophical argument is likely to seem pointless and misguided. As long as it does, a student is unlikely to have much success in participating in it by constructing his own arguments; but it is hard to imagine justifying the ends this appreciation presupposes without invoking one's experience of philosophical argumentation. End-intrinsic reasons for an end contrast with end-extrinsic reasons, reasons for an end that can be made intelligible and forceful to someone who does not already share it. Instrumental reasons are normally end-extrinsic: if my reason for adopting an end E is that it is a means of attaining a further end E', I can appreciate the force of this reason while having adopted only E', and not (yet) E. (I will not here consider whether end-intrinsic reasons are, despite the apparent circularity they involve, legitimate. What is important for present purposes is that, rightly or wrongly, we do engage in end-intrinsic justification of ends.)

Ends justified by end-intrinsic reasons are not the kind of thing you can just be argued into adopting, from the outside. Coming to have those ends involves meeting them halfway, tentatively adopting them in a way that allows you to see their point from the inside. The reasons adduced for them must make sense *as* reasons, and they cannot do this unless you somehow *already* share the ends they are reasons for. Now we make transitions like this often enough; but how are they possible? That is, how is it possible to adopt an end, for reasons, when those reasons presuppose having that very end?

When we look at the circumstances in which such things actually happen (and in particular, at the subset of such occurrences that we are inclined to consider reasonable changes in an agent's system of practical judgments), we often find friends on the scene. (Often but not always: I am not arguing that friendship is the only circumstance that will do the job.) It is often our friends who introduce us to new pursuits, pursuits whose point can only be appreciated from the inside.

> The prospect of having a baby had always left Florence cold. As a babysitter, she had seen how one's life becomes, as a matter of necessity, organized around this small, lumpy thing whose needs and desires are concrete, immediate, and irresistably urgent. She was quite aware that many other people find childrearing rewarding, and that it is quite often the focus of people's lives; and she had heard others trying to describe the intensity of their feeling for and attachment to their children. But she could only wonder at it.
>
> Then Florence spent some weeks staying with her sister and her sister's newborn infant. Seeing the baby through her sister's eyes, she could almost, she says, feel in her sister the pleasure she took in her child. Now she finds it much easier to see why everything else should pale in comparison. She has not decided to have a baby herself, but the option is live in a way it was not before; and she can now, in the right circumstances, wish babies on people she loves.[13]

One is inclined to give a friend the benefit of the doubt, as it were. That is a clumsy way of putting it, but there is, one way or another, something that looks like a presumption in favor of his practical judgments, simply because they are his. What kind of presumption is it, and why is it there?

Recall the way we are appropriating Aristotle's turn of phrase, giving it content by appeal to processes of deliberation. What it is for a friend to be 'another self' is for such things as the ends, attitudes, and so on, which jointly make up his 'self', to be treated in the same way that

---

13. I'm grateful to Jenann Ismael for this example and the next.

one treats the analogous items that make up one's *own* 'self'.[14] This allows us to explain the mediating role of friendship in the acquisition (or abandonment, or modification) of ends justified by end-intrinsic reasons: insofar as one treats one's friend's views in the way one treats one's own, they have the same kind of status that one's own views do. That is, one is willing to use them as bases for inference. But this puts one in a position to see the force of the end-intrinsic reasons that support the novel end under consideration; if one already *has*—in a perhaps tentative way—the end needed to render the reasons for it intelligible as reasons, one can then consider whether they are in fact *good* reasons; and if they are, one can then adopt the end in a full-fledged way, as entirely one's own.[15]

The objection was, it will be recalled, that one's accommodation of one's friend's desires could be accounted for by positing a background desire that his desires be satisfied. Now if one's sister loves her baby, such a background desire might underwrite helping her to take care of it. But it will not explain one's willingness and ability to reconsider the merits of

---

14. Of course, friendship is a matter of degree; the extent to which one stands in inferentially direct relations to one's friend's attitudes varies, both in respect of which attitudes one is directly related to, and in respect of the tightness, as it were, of the relation. I will return to this point below.

15. Once again, I'm not claiming that friendship is necessary for the acquisition of end-intrinsic reasons, or even that when it does play a role, the role I have described is always the one it plays. (I *am* suggesting that when we look, we will find that it often does play this role.) However, it's worth warning against dismissing friendship as an easily dispensable expedient in the acquisition of end-intrinsic reasons. Of the alternatives that I have found occur to people, most are ruled out by the arguments of chapter 2. Just wanting to learn from others, or to be open to and learn new things, and other motivations of that ilk, won't straightforwardly fit the bill: as we've seen, wanting to have an end doesn't mean you can actually come to have it, and we need to be shown how the gap between wanting and having can be bridged.

A somewhat different problem is presented by the idea that such bridges into the circle of ends and end-intrinsic reasons are not necessary because one can entertain reasons hypothetically. There are two difficulties with this response. First, it is one thing to think that *a* is a reason for *b*; it is another thing entirely to think that *a* would be a reason for *b* if one thought that *p*. Second, as Bernard Williams has pointed out, there are expressions of attitudes that must retain their force even when they are embedded in conditionals (1973b). If some of these can be end-intrinsic reasons, then they will remain inaccessible to the proposed hypothetical treatment.

childrearing as something one might want to do on one's own. Positing inferentially direct relations to her attitudes explains both.

Positing inferentially direct relations to the friend's attitudes also explains the way in which conflicts in ethical views are often addressed within the context of a friendship. Consider the following example.

> Gail and her roommate Harriet were fixing the fence in the backyard. Digging around the bottom of a post, they came across a line of ants. Harriet had gloves on, and, almost reflexively, reached down and started squashing them.
>
> Gail stopped her and insisted on an explanation, which turned out to be that Harriet hated insects. (Gail's demand for a moral justification probably did no more than convey her own contrary attitude: Harriet was not the type of person to think in terms of ethical argument from general principles, or to take the demand as a challenge to produce an articulated moral view.) Some time later, Gail saw Harriet catching a bee that had found its way into the house; she trapped it in a cup and, rather gingerly, carried it outside and let it go. Harriet had accepted Gail's conflicting practical judgment, and done so when she would have dismissively brushed off the objections of a stranger.

Note that I am not at the moment trying to justify the fact that, other things being equal, one takes one's friend's ethical and practical views more seriously than those of a stranger. I wish just now only to point out that it happens, and that it can be accounted for if we suppose that friends stand in inferentially direct relations to one another's practical judgments.

If a stranger's practical judgments differ from my own, this may not incline me to revise my own practical judgments. But if a friend's practical judgments conflict with mine, and if I treat his practical judgments as though they were my own—that is, if I treat them as a basis for inference—then I will experience the conflict as *internal;* and this is likely to prompt reconsideration and revision of my practical judgments in just the way my own second thoughts would. This account of the way friends can bring one to reconsider one's practical and ethical views is more responsible to the experience of such reconsideration than the obvious alternatives. One might suppose that Harriet must have reconsidered as a way of being nice to Gail, or because she did not want to alienate her. But had she done so, she would have been, in one way or another, humoring her friend; and although friends sometimes make the mistake of humoring each other, humoring a friend is precisely not taking him seriously. And, as we saw in Chapter 2, extrinsic reasons of this kind will not actually underwrite the assimilation of another's practical judgments into one's own take on things. Or one might be tempted to construe Harriet's second thoughts in terms of deference to Gail's ethical expertise; but Harriet need not have thought that Gail was any more knowledgeable about these things than she herself, and ethical expertise is perhaps less likely to prompt soul-searching than being taken to task by a friend is. (Harriet does not doubt that the Pope is intelligent and well-informed on moral matters, but she has no inclination whatsoever to reconsider her moral views when she realizes he disagrees with them.) In any case, the notion of moral expertise invoked by this alternative is itself dubious.[16] Now earlier I mentioned that because one's friends' ethical stances typically overlap with one's own, one might have reason to assume that their judgments would be those that one would make oneself; and this might be taken to provide reason to rely on them. (Similarity of judgment, that is, might stand in for moral expertise.) But recall that we are considering cases in which the ethical stances of friends conflict; these are precisely cases where the needed similarity is lacking.[17]

Now friends don't always take advice;[18] but one doesn't always pay attention to one's own second thoughts, either. And there is a reason that a friend's objections can feel like second rather than first thoughts. Because one does not typically stand in inferentially direct relations to all

---

16. The arguments in play pull in different directions at this point. On the one hand, practical inductions underwritten by practical observations seem to allow for ethical expertise as a genuine possibility. On the other hand, the precise extent of the intersubjectivity of practical observation is an empirical question—and we have on hand, interestingly enough, an a priori argument to the effect that it cannot cover the whole of the practical sphere (note 18, section 2.4).

17. But still, might not there be alternative explanations for, and construals of, the ways in which we take disagreements with our friends into account? I will return briefly to this point in note 32; it will turn out not to matter if there are.

18. This objection is due to Jill Eskenazi.

one's friend's attitudes, the attitudes to which one does stand in inferentially direct relations can, lacking the other beliefs, practical judgments and so on that cohere with them in the friend's mental life, strike one as a little like isolated hunches: views that have a degree of initial plausibility, but nothing like the robust assurance that is more likely to (but need not) accompany a view of one's own.

If your friend disagrees with you on an ethical or practical point, this does not mean that you must abandon your view for his. You can examine your friend's reasons for having his view, and the plausibility of the other views (your own and your friend's) with which it must fit. You can decide that his view conflicts with things that you already think or want, and is to be rejected. But—and this is the point—there is a presumption in favor of hanging onto his view, and integrating it into your system of practical judgments, simply because it is a view that, in a sense, you *already have;* this presumption will be expressed in attempts to reconcile the conflicting views. The inferentially direct relations friends stand in to each others' attitudes explain, as background desires for the satisfaction of friends' desires cannot, the ways in which friends often address conflict between their ethical stances.[19]

Standing in inferentially direct relations to a friend's practical judgments supplies one with premises for one's practical inductions. My own experience with Chantal Ackerman films is too restricted for me to be willing to generalize from it. But my friend has opinions, mostly positive, about a number of them, and on the basis of *Jeanne Dielman,* which I have seen, and the others with which she is familiar, I am willing to go to an Ackerman film that neither of us has seen. Friendship plays an important, if hard to pin down, role here: I know that opinions on Ackerman films differ dramatically, and that most people find them merely

---

19. If practical judgments can conflict in a way analogous to the way a system of beliefs can prove inconsistent, then there is also a practical analog of a further form of theoretical reasoning: the resolution of contradictions in one's system of beliefs. (I'm grateful to Candace Vogler for this idea. Because the topic of this book is empirical practical reasoning, I will not explore these issues further here; for preliminary remarks, see Millgram and Thagard, 1996.) However, if this is right, then in cases where I internalize a friend's practical judgments, and these conflict with my own, I may be put in the position of doing reasoning of this kind.

tedious; and I am willing to disregard the testimony of most people in favor of my friend's. Once again, a desire for the satisfaction of my friend's desires does not explain my willingness to use those desires—or, more accurately, the assessments that give body to those desires—as bases for inferences to general conclusions that will control my own actions.

Finally, notice that each of these ways in which a friend can influence one's system of practical judgments tends to bring about points of convergence between one's own system of practical judgments and the friend's. Coming to see the end-intrinsic reasons for a friend's ends will make it more likely, although of course not inevitable, that one adopt those ends for oneself. Trying to resolve a conflict between a friend's practical judgments and one's own, in the way that one does when the conflict is internal, is, again, likely to bring one to agreement with one's friend—particularly if the process is symmetrical. And lastly, if friends share the premises of their practical inductions, they will be more likely to share the general practical judgments that are the conclusions of their inductions.

§ 7.6

I will now turn to some features of friendship remarked upon by Aristotle, and indicate the ways in which inferentially direct relations can account for them. To begin with, one desires the good for one's friend for the friend's own sake (that is, without ulterior motives); and one loves one's friend for his virtues. It is worth noting that these two facts are connected. One's friend's good is not something independent of his ends: desiring the good for one's friend requires being able to endorse a suitable portion of those ends, to wish him well, and to be willing to aid and abet him in their pursuit.[20] And this requires taking those ends to be at least reasonable, if not clearly meriting pursuit. That is, it has

---

20. One's friend's good is, of course, not simply the aggregate of his ends; we can in fact think that a friend's good is incompatible with the fulfillment of particular ends he pursues. One might have a view on which a person's good can be largely independent of what he takes his goals to be, but I do not think this to be a very plausible view; possibly the right thing to say in cases where the putative good does not involve any, or very many, of the agent's ends is that such a person fails to have a good at all. Suffice it for now that in such circumstances the extremely patronizing attitude required by wanting for someone

to be possible to have the sort of respect for one's friend's ends that is continuous with regarding him as virtuous, if one is to desire his good in the way that is characteristic of friendship.

Aristotle's way of putting the second claim, that one loves one's friend for his virtue, may have an unfortunately preachy sound, but it is nonetheless common sense. Asked why one loves so-and-so, a description of his character showing him in a certain kind of favorable light is a perfectly reasonable response. (This description need not highlight the traditional list of virtues, of course, and it need not make him out to be a moral person in the usual sense, provided one does not oneself find the traditional virtues overridingly important.) Now, this commonplace is often construed in roughly the following way: the fact that a certain person has praiseworthy properties—where it is understood that these properties are judged to be praiseworthy independently of the friendship—is one's reason for adopting toward him the attitudes of friendship (among which is the desire for the friend's good for his own sake).[21]

While I believe that the view that one loves one's friend for his virtues should be taken seriously, this way of construing it will not do. First, if one's friend's virtues are simply praiseworthy properties, they do not explain why *that* person is being befriended rather than the many other virtuous people one might find. This kind of account is consequently unable to accommodate the loyalty that is also a central aspect of friendship: why does one not abandon one's current friend when more virtuous substitutes happen along?[22] To love a friend is to treat him as something other than a fungible commodity, even when the commodity is as rarified as a bearer of certain virtues; and again, on this construal it is not clear how this is possible.

Second, this construal fails to account for the way in which friends take seriously practical judgments that are not already shared. While it may explain the fact that, in order to be someone's friend, you must

---

a good so divergent from his conception of it would not normally be compatible with friendship.

21. For a recent piece of work in this vein, see Whiting, 1991.

22. The reader will recognize the problem to be structurally identical to the one encountered in the example in section 2.2.

approve of and endorse a sufficiently large proportion of his ends, if some of his ends are not already intelligible *as ends* to you, if some of his practical judgments are contrary to those you yourself hold, these are, on the construal at hand, simply points on which you differ. There need be no tendency to adopt his views and ends beyond that which you would have toward someone you regarded as a generally well-informed and reliable stranger. But, as we saw in the previous section, such a tendency is not infrequently a prominent aspect of friendship.

Third, recall that *apparent* virtue will generally consist in the agreement of another's ethical (or, more broadly, practical) stance with one's own.[23] On the construal we are considering of the claim that one loves one's friend for his virtues, it seems to follow that the more a person is like you, the better a candidate for friendship he is; and the points on which your respective practical judgments disagree will simply be impediments or obstructions to the friendship. On this view, that is, the ideal friend would be a spiritual clone. And this seems to ignore the fact that we value and take seriously the ways in which our friends differ from us, even (or especially) when it comes to our respective practical (and ethical) judgments.[24]

We can address these problems by altering the direction of explanation. Let us take the inferentially direct relation one has to the friend's attitudes as explanatorily basic.[25] We have already seen a number of ways in which inferentially direct relations to a friend's attitudes bring about change in one's system of practical judgments. We can now appeal to this

---

23. In some cases, the internal tensions in one's own ethical stance may complicate matters; for example, one may take virtue to consist in agreement with an ideal the acknowledgment of which is part of one's ethical stance, but to which one does not oneself live up.

24. Some of the ways we value these differences have first-person counterparts: it is important to be of several minds on some matters, to be drawn in different directions by competing self-conceptions, and so on. But only some: even if the friend is 'another self', it is important to remember that the friend is an *other* self. One can hold a friend's hand, but not one's own.

25. In saying that, I don't mean to suggest that there are not in turn psychological explanations of such inferentially direct relations; what is taken for granted in one context of explanation may be the object of explanation in another. (I'm grateful to Rachana Kamtekar for pressing me on this point.)

account to explain one's desire for the friend's good, the phenomenon of ethical respect, and the intimate connection between them.

In the last section, we saw how standing in inferentially direct relations to another's practical judgments can bring about revision in one's own, when the two sets of judgments diverge. Now when friends' judgments diverge, the adjustment is likely to be mutual. And in that case, the inferentially direct relations one stands in to the friend's practical judgments are likely to contribute significantly to one's perceiving the friend as virtuous. For suppose that one's ethical stance were to diverge from the friend's at some point. The reconsideration prompted by finding this conflict between the friend's view (which is being treated much like one's own) and one's own would then tend to bring about convergence on that point, in ways we have already discussed. (I say 'tend' because, if an issue is not particularly urgent, it may not benefit from such reconsideration any more than less-than-urgent internal conflicts; because friends can part ways on particular issues and remain friends; because particular issues can bring about the parting of friends; and because friends may choose to table particularly contentious issues for the sake of preserving the friendship.) And since one tends to regard those with whom one agrees on ethical matters as virtuous, one's friend will come to seem to one to be more and more virtuous. Partly this will be because one's friend is changing—because he is *becoming,* by one's own standards, more virtuous. But partly it is because one's own conception of virtue is changing: because one is developing an understanding of virtue that is tailored to the friend.

In the course of this process, one becomes more able to endorse one's friend's ends whole-heartedly. Not only does one stand in an inferentially direct relation to many of the friend's desires and other attitudes; but the conflicts between his view of the good and one's own are, to an ever-increasing degree, resolved. This in turn makes the characteristic attitude of friendship, desiring the good for the friend for his own sake, straightforward and natural; for while the friend's good is not simply the aggregate of the objects of his desires, those objects of desire are, by and large, elements of it.

The relation, then, of virtue to friend is not that of a standard antecedently possessed applied to prospective candidates; one does not go around with one's template, choosing one's friends from those who match it most closely. Rather, the standard of virtue shapes itself to fit the person to whom it is applied. In this way, the inferentially direct relation one stands in to the friend's attitudes, and the adjustments in one's own ethical stance that it informs, jointly underwrite (in part, and gradually) both ethical respect for one's friend, and one's desiring the good for the friend for his own sake: if you endorse his ends, you're well on your way to respecting the person who has them, and you're well on your way to desiring the good that they in part constitute.

Another feature of friendship mentioned by Aristotle is its exclusivity—the fact that one cannot have very many close friends. (The Hollywood star who throws a party and invites only five hundred of her *very* closest friends is amusing because she seems not to know, or care, what friends are.) On the view that takes friendship to be a response to independently identified virtue, it is hard to see why not: why *not* count as many virtuous acquaintances as I can find as my friends? Now the account of how one's understanding of virtue is shaped by friendship goes a good way towards resolving this problem; if my idea of virtue is tailored, over the course of the history of a friendship, to fit my friend, it is not surprising that it does not fit many others well. In any case, if inferentially direct relations to the friend's practical judgments are taken as central to and characteristic of love or friendship, this exclusivity is necessary: one cannot expect to maintain a coherently organized personality while treating the attitudes of very many other people as though they were one's own.[26] This reconstruction of the feature does not in itself answer the question: how many friends can one have? But it does reduce it to questions about the coherence of different patterns of motivation.[27]

---

26. One might think that the problem is simply that one doesn't have enough *time* for very many friends. But the two difficulties are not as distinct as it might at first seem. The problem of maintaining a coherently organized personality is the problem of doing so in a world where you don't have time to do everything. Unified agency is a matter of choices that are fitted to one another, and choice is only necessary when, because you can't have it both ways, you have to choose.

27. There are further features of friendship which the present view shows promise of accommodating; I will quickly sketch a couple. One notable feature of friendship is its relative permanence. We are inclined to think, of extremely transitory friendships,

§ 7.7

Let's take stock of the argument to this point. I've reconstructed a number of features often found in friendship, using the apparatus of inferentially direct relations to another's mental states. It's important to note, however, that there are familiar characteristics of friendship that I have not reconstructed, most notably, the simple fact that one *likes* one's friend and his company. (The discussion in the previous chapter suggests that this must be bound up with judgments of desirability that are almost inevitable within the context of a friendship, but I am not confident that I can explain what these are or why they are inevitable.) Other such characteristics include the intimacy possible in friendship, the willingness of friends to think better of one than one does oneself, and the expectation that among friends we can be ourselves.[28] And while I have partially explained the importance of shared history in a friendship, I do not think the explanation I have managed is more than partial.

Perhaps some of these lacunae might be handled by natural extensions of the account under consideration. Empathy, our disposition to

---

that they were not really friendships after all. And full-fledged friendships tend to last, although of course there are no guarantees that any particular friendship will weather the difficulties it runs into. I won't attempt a full explanation of this fact here; but notice that the account I have been developing, in assimilating aspects of friendship to features of synchronic personal identity, suggests assimilating the durability of friendship to the durability, as one is tempted to put it, of diachronic personal identity.

The problem of explaining how, if one loves a friend for his virtues, one does not love all virtuous people, or at any rate, all of one's virtuous acquaintances, has been partially addressed, but the problem has a remainder. Suppose we imagine, in the manner of philosophical science fiction, a duplicator that reproduces one's friend with all his virtues. Why, then, does one love one's friend and not the duplicate? (Or does one?) I don't want to try to solve the remainder of the problem now; it suffices to suggest the resources the present account provides for dealing with this difficulty. If Cindy and Mindy are duplicates, I can stand in inferentially direct relations to Cindy's attitudes without being so related to Mindy's, in just the way that I can stand in inferentially direct relations to my own attitudes without being so related to the attitudes of a duplicate of myself.

28. Kant, 1930/1980, pp. 205f, emphasized the fact that one can confide in one's friends. Cf. also Kant, 1797/1986, Ak. 472. The second point is expressed by a character in *The Philadelphia Story;* I'm grateful to Stanley Cavell for drawing my attention to it. And Garrett Deckel and Harold Langsam reminded me of the third.

feel our friends' emotions as though they were our own, is central to friendship; and if one's friend likes himself, then if one empathizes, one will like one's friend as well. But while empathy is of a piece with our disposition to treat our friends' practical judgments as our own, I will not now try to integrate it into the present account. The reason is that the account is inference-based, and we are still lacking an adequate understanding of the inferential role played by the emotions.

In any case, my primary purpose here has not been to develop a complete reconstruction of friendship in terms of inferentially direct relations to one's friend's mental states, nor has my concern been to show that a relationship in which inferentially direct relations to another's attitudes do not figure is not friendship. Rather, I have been trying to show that primitive trust in practical testimony—standing in inferentially direct relations to another's mental states—tends to generate characteristic features of friendship: that is, that the people you trust, and who trust you back, will tend to end up your friends.[29]

That we do not trust just anybody is a fairly straightforward upshot of basic features of the territory of practical reasoning. By contrast, what are usually treated as the paradigm cases of theoretical reasoning and knowledge are characterized by a high degree of intersubjectivity, and this allows a kind of promiscuity of trust. If it is normally alright for so-and-so to believe that p when it would be alright for me to believe that p, then, if I don't have any reason to think that so-and-so doesn't

---

29. Let me, however, indicate in what way these arguments do lean toward the idea that friendship centrally involves inferentially direct relations to the friend's attitudes. By this I mean not that there is a list of necessary conditions for friendship, and that we would not call anything friendship that did not satisfy them. (Why should it matter that something satisfies all the conditions on some list, rather than the conditions on some slightly shorter list? Does it matter that, by definition, only something that satisfies the conditions on the former list is *called* friendship?) Rather, even though it is incomplete, the account at hand suggests that central features of friendship are mutually explanatory, and mutually content-determining. Inferentially direct relations explain both one's non-instrumental desire for one's friend's good, and one's ethical respect for him; they do this by determining in significant part what one finds worth desiring and what worthy of respect. Consequently, standing in inferentially direct relations to the friend's attitudes is not just an item on an arbitrary list of stipulative conditions for calling something a friendship; for were it removed, the remaining items on the list would have such different content that it would be a mistake to think of them as remaining the same conditions.

know about p, or that he's going to lie to me, I can just take his word for it that p: in such cases, a suitably accredited theoretical judgment for one person is a suitably accredited theoretical judgment for another.[30] One of the prominent features of the domain of practical deliberation is, by contrast, the lack of this kind of convergence: someone's mother may advise him, on the basis of her painfully acquired experience, that fulfillment is to be found in bare-knuckled bond trading, but this may be advice that his own experience contradicts. If people's practical views (quite properly) diverge, then if you trust everyone, you will end up with an incoherent set of practical judgments, one that is not a suitable guide to action. The job of practical reasoning is to guide action, and if practical reasoning is to do its job, one's acceptance of practical testimony cannot be indiscriminate.

This leaves us with the question of whom to trust, and it might seem that we have answered this question: you trust your friends. But this would be to get the direction of explanation in the argument I have been developing backward. Suppose it to be in fact the case that inferentially direct relations to one's friend's attitudes are constitutive of friendship (or of certain kinds of friendship). Then it is not as though one can first identify one's friends, and then use that information to figure out whom to trust about what. Rather, whom you trust, and about what, and how far, determines who your friends are, and what kind of friends they are. (Compare: one doesn't figure out whom to like by first identifying one's friends, and then making up one's mind to like them; liking someone is part of being their friend.[31]) And in any case, no argument has been given that you should trust the particular people who happen to be your friends, or that you should trust them further than you have trusted

30. As I indicated in the previous chapter, I am not at all certain that what are usually treated as the paradigm cases of theoretical reasoning and knowledge—roughly, science and statements about medium-sized dry goods—are the whole of, or even typical of, the territory of theoretical reasoning. So the contrast I am drawing, while helpful for exposition, is far more straightforward than the one I would need to draw if I were to amend the received view here to my own. Even with these complications, however, something of this contrast would survive; see note 18, section 2.4.

31. This point has been emphasized by Jennifer Whiting, in the course of an argument for a somewhat different point of similarity between friendship and personal identity (1986).

them already. That those whom you trust are likely to end up your friends does not show that those who end up your friends are worthy of your trust.[32]

This means that I have left entirely open questions such as: Whom should one befriend? How do friendships begin, and how do they deepen? And is the process one that can be described as rational or irrational? This last question might seem an odd concern to import into considerations regarding friendship, since most people think of such processes as matters of personal inclination rather than deliberation. But if the present account is on target, the question is quite pressing: in beginning and deepening (at any rate a certain kind of) friendship, one is making the mental states of another, in the sense that most matters for rationality, literally one's own. If one is going to use another's mental states as bases for inference, surely, one might think, there must be rationality constraints on when another's mental states can be adopted in this way. However, I won't consider these questions further here.

What we have shown is that we are committed to the legitimacy of primitive trust in practical testimony. Just as showing we were committed to the legitimacy of practical induction did not tell us which practical inductions we should make, so this conclusion says nothing about which practical testimony we should trust. But trust in practical testimony has, as its natural upshot, some of the central structural features of friendship. (In particular cases, of course, it may result in relationships we would want to distinguish from friendship; as in the mentoring of an apprentice, for instance.) And this suggests that love or friendship is more closely related to the traditionally central concerns of epistemology and ethics than it has usually been taken to be.[33]

---

32. This is an occasion to defuse lingering objections to my claims about the ways in which friends treat disagreements, end-intrinsic reasons for goals, and so on. Once again, the issue is one of the direction of explanation: instead of arguing that friendship requires trust of this kind, I am arguing that trust of this kind tends to generate friendships. (Trust has been argued to be required not by the context of friendship, but as a precondition for unity of agency.) In those friendships that *are* generated in this way, the construals I have given of how conflicts and disagreements are treated will be largely correct. But I make no claims with respect to friendships of other kinds.

33. The view I have been developing is also a corrective to attitudes that now seem to be deeply entrenched in the popular culture. While there are some things that you have to

By way of illustration, we can use this account of friendship to motivate the thought that we should not take impartiality in ethics for granted. There is a widespread presumption that the correct moral theory must treat everyone alike, and require moral agents to do the same. And although there has been occasional dissent,[34] what concessions there have been to partiality have not made them basic to the theory. (For example, consequentialist theories may allow that it produces better consequences if people take care of their own; but in drawing this conclusion, the consequences are assessed impartially.)

We have seen, however, that what practical reasons a person has are closely connected with whom he trusts and loves. Everyone cannot have the same friends and parents, and so people will be working with different initial systems of practical judgments. Among these inherited reasons for action will be practical judgments whose adoption will tend toward partiality; to treat my friend's ends as a direct basis for inference, but not a stranger's, is to be partial to my friend. Partiality appears at the ground level of practical rationality: for unified agency to be possible, different things must count as practical reasons for different people. This is not yet a conclusive argument that ethical theory must not be impartial; there is room for many changes of direction between an account of practical rationality and the final shape of one's moral theory. But I think it does show that we need to take seriously the possibility that evenhandedness will not turn out to be a deep feature of the right moral theory.

Of course, that a theory of practical reasoning might have partialist tendencies is nothing new: I suggested in the introduction that a good part of the history of moral theory is made of attempts to resist the partialist tendencies of instrumentalism. That resistance is understandable, if the alternative to a uniform evenhandedness is the single-minded pursuit of one's unregulated desires. But if that is not what partiality amounts to—as, on the present account, it need not—then perhaps it does not have to be so strenuously, and so reflexively, resisted.

---

learn for yourself, and some things about which you do have to make up your mind for yourself, there are also circumstances in which there is nothing wrong with attending to authority.

34. See, for example, Williams, 1981b.

8

Conclusion

I have argued that instrumental reasoning cannot be all the practical reasoning there is, and that practical induction is a legitimate form of inference. I have further argued that there are practical versions of observation and testimony that supply the premises for practical inductions, and I used this fact to develop accounts of pleasure and friendship. It remains to make one last retrospective point about the status of the argument for these conclusions: that, because we have been asking how we *have to* reason, the argument has itself been a practical argument. What this comes to can be brought out by considering a couple of skeptical responses to it.[1]

That argument proceeded by showing that practical induction is necessary to sustain unity of agency. Novelty is pervasive, and if you do not learn new priorities, interests, and concerns from experience, you will prove incapable of responding coherently to the surprises that inevitably come your way. This recapitulation of the argument may make it seem vulnerable to skepticism about one's stake in the practical side of one's

---

1. The point of considering skepticism now is not to refute it. While I have tried to show that, if one is engaged in practical reasoning, then practical induction is a legitimate way to go about it, it has not been my concern here to prove that it makes sense, always or even ever, to try to figure out what to do—although, because the question, whether I should try to figure out what to do, is itself practical, by the time it arises, an affirmative answer to one somewhat minimal version of it has already been presupposed.

own personhood: what if I don't care about the unity, coherence, or over-all success of my own agency?

I remarked earlier that the question of how to think is a practical question. On a view that takes practical questions to be questions about how to attain your goals, the question turns out to be: what ways of thinking will get you results that you happen to want?[2] But we have rejected instrumentalism, and with it, the means to insist on this way of construing the question. And in fact I have not tried to show that we engage in practical induction as a means to the end of being unified agents; rather, I have argued that the legitimacy of practical induction must be presupposed by agents. There is an Aristotelian shorthand for the contrast I want to draw: my argument traces out (part of) the formal cause of agency. It does not, except when making use of the dispensable fiction of an agent's designer, purport to exhibit its final cause.

Consequently, this skeptical response gets the direction of argument backward. Rather than first determining whether one wants to be an agent, and using that to settle the legitimacy of practical induction, one ought to use practical induction to investigate the stake one has in one's own agency. If one's experience of coherent and effective activity is, as a rule, rewarding, one might learn, by practical induction, that the unity of one's own agency matters a good deal to one; and if it is not, one might learn the contrary. This very personal question must be investi-gated largely on a case-by-case basis.

There is another, related form that skepticism directed toward the ar-gument we are looking back at can take, and that is doubt as to whether unity of agency is possible. If unity of agency is beyond our reach, then the question of what is required to sustain it might seem to have been preempted. There are two aspects of unity of agency in play in the ar-gument, and so such skepticism can take either of two forms: you can

---

2. Stich, 1990, ch. 6, claims that this is the right way to argue about which cognitive techniques are correct. But this method of settling questions about rationality simply takes the practical adequacy of a particular cognitive technique—means-end reasoning—entirely for granted. I am inclined to think that the method only seemed plausible in the first place because it was not being applied to the domain of practical inference. Applied there, it turns out to be ineffective, for roughly the reasons canvassed in Chapter 2, and, because effectiveness is of the essence when it comes to getting what one wants, is consequently self-refuting.

doubt that your agency will extend forward through time (skepticism about diachronic unity of agency), or you can doubt that you are a unified agent *now* (skepticism about synchronic unity of agency). I want to suggest that the first of these options is live in a way that the second is not.

If you are to execute your plan, you must be around when the time comes to do so. But you might suspect, or know, that you won't be. You might be run over by a bus later this week, and so not be in a position to go through with your plan the week after next. (To rehearse the earlier argument: *within* the context of planning for the week after next, you must assume that you will not have been killed by a bus in the meantime—just as you must assume that you will be a unified agent. This doesn't entail that you won't be killed by a bus, and it doesn't entail that you don't need to take steps to make sure that you won't be . . . in this case, very rapid steps out of the path of the oncoming bus.) You certainly will not be around two thousand years hence. Or, in a less dramatic key, you may be fairly sure that you will not stick with your decisions, or carry them through sensibly. In such cases, the appropriate response is to allow the borders of your agency to circumscribe your plans.

Consequently, full-fledged skepticism about diachronic unity of agency is a view with practical consequences. These are, roughly, that you should live in the moment, and not bother to make any long-range plans. Of course, if these are your circumstances, you should not assume that this is a policy you could *adhere* to: the import of the practical conclusion is of quite limited scope. But it is a practical conclusion nonetheless.

However, full-fledged skepticism about *synchronic* unity of agency is a view with no practical consequences: if it is true, there is nothing you can do about it, because there is nothing that will amount to your decision as to what to do (or, equivalently, because there is—practically speaking—no *you* to do the deciding). And so skepticism about one's unity of agency at the present moment is practically unimportant. One might as well dismiss the possibility and proceed on the assumption that it is false, in the same way, and for the same reasons, that one can, in the course of one's theoretical reasonings, dismiss the possibility that one has no mind and is not really thinking.

References

Anscombe, G. E. M. 1981. Authority in morals. In *Ethics, Religion and Politics: Collected Philosophical Papers*, vol. 3, pp. 43–50. Oxford: Basil Blackwell.

———. 1985. *Intention*. 2d ed. Ithaca: Cornell University Press.

Audi, R. 1989. *Practical Reasoning*. New York: Routledge.

Austin, J. L. 1979. Other minds. In J. O. Urmson and G. J. Warnock, eds., *Philosophical Papers*, 3d ed., pp. 76–116. Oxford: Oxford University Press.

Baier, A. 1986. Trust and anti-trust. *Ethics, 96,* 231–260.

Barry, D. 1990. *Dave Barry Turns 40*. New York: Fawcett Columbine.

Bentham, J. 1789/1973. An introduction to the principles of morals and legislation. In *The Utilitarians*, pp. 7–398. New York: Anchor Press.

Braithwaite, R. B. 1953/1974. The predictionist justification of induction. In R. Swinburne, ed., *The Justification of Induction*, pp. 102–126. Oxford: Oxford University Press.

Brandt, R. 1979. *A Theory of the Good and the Right*. Oxford: Clarendon Press.

Bratman, M. 1987. *Intention, Plans, and Practical Reason*. Cambridge, Mass.: Harvard University Press.

———. 1992. Planning and the stability of intention. *Minds and Machines, 2,* 1–16.

Broadie, S. W. 1987. The problem of practical intellect in Aristotle's ethics. In J. Cleary, ed., *Proceedings of the Boston Area Colloquium in Ancient Philosophy,* vol. 3, pp. 229–252. Lanham: University Press of America.

Cherniak, C. 1986. *Minimal Rationality*. Cambridge, Mass.: MIT Press.

Coady, C. A. J. 1992. *Testimony*. Oxford: Clarendon Press.

Collins, A. W. 1987. *The Nature of Mental Things.* Notre Dame, Ind.: University of Notre Dame Press.

Cook, J. T. 1987. Deciding to believe without self-deception. *Journal of Philosophy, 84(8),* 441–446.

Davidson, D., McKinsey, J. C. C., and Suppes, P. 1955. Outlines of a formal theory of value, I. *Philosophy of Science, 22(2),* 140–160.

Dennett, D. 1984. *Elbow Room: The Varieties of Free Will Worth Wanting.* Cambridge, Mass.: MIT Press.

———. 1991. *Consciousness Explained.* Boston: Little, Brown and Co.

Dick, P. K. 1990. We can remember it for you wholesale. In *The Collected Short Stories of Philip K. Dick,* vol. 2, pp. 35–52. New York: Carol Publishing Group.

Dohrn-van Rossum, G. 1996. *History of the Hour: Clocks and Modern Temporal Orders.* Chicago: University of Chicago Press. Trans. Thomas Dunlap.

Dummett, M. 1973. *Frege: Philosophy of Language.* London: Duckworth.

Fisher, M. F. K. 1990. *The Art of Eating.* New York: Macmillan.

Fleischacker, S. 1994. *The Ethics of Culture.* Ithaca: Cornell University Press.

Frankfurt, H. 1988. Freedom of the will and the concept of a person. In *The Importance of What We Care About,* pp. 11–25. Cambridge: Cambridge University Press.

Gibbard, A. 1990. *Wise Choices, Apt Feelings: A Theory of Normative Judgment.* Cambridge, Mass.: Harvard University Press.

Goodman, N. 1979. *Fact, Fiction and Forecast.* 3rd ed. Indianapolis: Hackett.

Gosling, J. C. B. 1969. *Pleasure and Desire: The Case for Hedonism Reviewed.* Oxford: Clarendon Press.

Hardwig, J. 1985. Epistemic dependence. *Journal of Philosophy, 82(7),* 335–349.

Harman, G. 1976. Practical reasoning. *Review of Metaphysics, 29(3),* 431–463.

———. 1993. Desired desires. In R. Frey and C. Morris, eds., *Value, Welfare, and Morality,* pp. 138–157. Cambridge: Cambridge University Press.

Hoffer, E. 1966. *The True Believer: Thoughts on the Nature of Mass Movements.* New York: Perennial Library.

Holland, J., Holyoak, K., Nisbet, R., and Thagard, P. 1986. *Induction: Processes of Inference, Learning, and Discovery.* Cambridge, Mass.: MIT Press.

Hurley, S. 1989. *Natural Reasons: Personality and Polity.* Oxford: Oxford University Press.

Ishiguro, K. 1989. *The Remains of the Day.* New York: Vintage.

James, W. 1896/1961. The will to believe. In *Essays in Pragmatism*, pp. 88–109. New York: Hafner.

Jeffrey, R. 1974. Preferences among preferences. *Journal of Philosophy, 71*, 377–391.

Kant, I. 1785/1981. *Grounding for the Metaphysics of Morals*. Indianapolis: Hackett. Trans. James Ellington.

———. 1797/1986. Metaphysical principles of virtue. In *Ethical Philosophy*, Book 2, pp. 31–161. Indianapolis: Hackett. Trans. James Ellington.

———. 1930/1980. *Lectures on Ethics*. Indianapolis: Hackett. Trans. Louis Infield.

Katz, L. 1986. *Hedonism as Metaphysics of Mind and Value*. PhD diss., Princeton University.

Kavka, G. 1983. The toxin puzzle. *Analysis, 43(1)*, 33–36.

Kolnai, A. 1978. Deliberation is of ends. In F. Dunlop and B. Klug, eds., *Ethics, Value and Reality: Selected Papers of Aurel Kolnai*, pp. 44–62. Indianapolis: Hackett.

Korsgaard, C. 1990. *The Standpoint of Practical Reason*. New York: Garland.

Kuhn, T. 1970. *The Structure of Scientific Revolutions*. Chicago: University of Chicago Press.

Lear, J. 1990. *Love and Its Place in Nature*. New York: Farrar, Straus and Giroux.

Lewis, D. 1989. Dispositional theories of value. *Proceedings of the Aristotelian Society Supplement, 63*, 113–137.

Luce, R. D. and Raiffa, H. 1957. *Games and Decisions*. New York: John Wiley and Sons.

Mackie, J. L. 1976. *Problems from Locke*. Oxford: Clarendon Press.

———. 1983. *Ethics: Inventing Right and Wrong*. New York: Penguin.

McDowell, J. 1980. Meaning, communication, and knowledge. In Z. van Straaten, ed., *Philosophical Subjects: Essays Presented to P. F. Strawson*, pp. 117–139. Oxford: Clarendon Press.

———. 1985. Values and secondary qualities. In T. Honderich, ed., *Morality and Objectivity*, pp. 110–129. London: Routledge and Kegan Paul.

McGinn, C. 1983. *The Subjective View*. Oxford: Clarendon Press.

Meiland, J. 1980. What ought we to believe? or the ethics of belief revisited. *American Philosophical Quarterly, 17(1)*, 15–24.

Mill, J. S. 1861/1969. Utilitarianism. In J. M. Robson, ed., *Essays on Ethics, Religion and Society: Collected Works of John Stuart Mill*, vol. 10, pp. 203–259. Toronto: University of Toronto Press/Routledge and Kegan Paul.

Millgram, E. 1987. Aristotle on making other selves. *Canadian Journal of Philosophy, 17(2),* 361–376.

———. 1991. Harman's hardness arguments. *Pacific Philosophical Quarterly, 72(3),* 181–202.

———. 1995a. Inhaltsreiche ethische Begriffe und die Unterscheidung zwischen Tatsachen und Werten. In C. Fehige and G. Meggle, eds., *Zum moralischen Denken,* pp. 354–388. Frankfurt a.M.: Suhrkamp.

———. 1995b. Was Hume a Humean? *Hume Studies, 21(1),* 75–93.

———. 1996. Williams' argument against external reasons. *Nous, 30(2),* 197–220.

———. 1997a. Incommensurability and practical reasoning. In R. Chang, ed., *Incommensurability and Value.* Cambridge, Mass.: Harvard University Press.

———. 1997b. Varieties of practical reasoning. In G. Meggle and P. Steinacker, eds., *Analyomen 2: Proceedings of the 2nd Conference 'Perspectives in Analytical Philosophy'.* Berlin: de Gruyter.

Millgram, E. and Thagard, P. 1996. Deliberative coherence. *Synthese, 108(1),* 63–88.

Nagel, T. 1978. *The Possibility of Altruism.* Princeton: Princeton University Press.

Nell, O. 1974. *Acting on Principle.* New York: Columbia University Press.

Nozick, R. 1989. *The Examined Life.* New York: Simon and Schuster.

Nussbaum, M. 1986. *The Fragility of Goodness: Luck and Ethics in Greek Tragedy and Philosophy.* Cambridge: Cambridge University Press.

Peirce, C. S. 1877/1955. The fixation of belief. In J. Buchler, ed., *Philosophical Writings of Peirce,* pp. 5–22, New York: Dover.

Peterson, C., Maier, S., and Seligman, M. 1993. *Learned Helplessness.* Oxford: Oxford University Press.

Prior, A. N. 1960. The runabout inference-ticket. *Analysis, 21(2),* 38–39.

Quinn, W. 1993. *Morality and Action.* Cambridge: Cambridge University Press.

Raphael, D. D. 1969. *British Moralists 1650–1800.* Oxford: Clarendon Press.

Richardson, H. 1994. *Practical Reasoning about Final Ends.* Cambridge: Cambridge University Press.

Ross, A. 1986. Why do we believe what we're told? *Ratio, 28(1),* 69–88.

Ryle, G. 1954. *Dilemmas.* Cambridge: Cambridge University Press.

Salmon, W. 1974. The pragmatic justification of induction. In R. Swinburne, ed., *The Justification of Induction,* pp. 85–97. Oxford: Oxford University Press.

Schaper, E. 1987. The pleasures of taste. In E. Schaper, ed., *Pleasure, Preference and Value: Studies in Philosophical Aesthetics,* pp. 39–56. Cambridge: Cambridge University Press.

Schmidtz, D. 1995. *Rational Choice and Moral Agency.* Princeton: Princeton University Press.

Shoemaker, S. 1963. *Self-Knowledge and Self-Identity.* Ithaca: Cornell University Press.

————. 1997. Desiring at will (and at pill). A reply to Millgram. In C. Fehige and U. Wessels, eds., *Preferences,* pp. 26–32. Berlin: de Gruyter.

Sidgwick, H. 1907/1981. *The Methods of Ethics.* Indianapolis: Hackett.

Somerville, A. 1993. *Fields of Greens.* New York: Bantam Books.

Stalker, D. 1994. *Grue! The New Riddle of Induction.* La Salle: Open Court Publishing Company.

Stich, S. 1983. *From Folk Psychology to Cognitive Science: The Case Against Belief.* Cambridge, Mass.: MIT Press.

————. 1990. *The Fragmentation of Reason: Preface to a Pragmatic Theory of Cognitive Evaluation.* Cambridge, Mass.: MIT Press.

Stroud, B. 1989. The study of human nature and the subjectivity of value. *The Tanner Lectures on Human Values,* 9, 213–259.

Thagard, P. 1993. Computational tractability and conceptual coherence: Why do computer scientists believe that P ≠ NP? *Canadian Journal of Philosophy,* 23, 349–364.

Thagard, P. and Millgram, E. 1995. Inference to the best plan: A coherence theory of decision. In D. Leake and A. Ram, eds., *Goal-Driven Learning,* pp. 439–454. Cambridge, Mass.: MIT Press.

Watterson, B. 1993. *The Days are Just Packed.* Kansas City: Andrews and McMeel.

Welbourne, M. 1986. *The Community of Knowledge.* Aberdeen: Aberdeen University Press.

Whiting, J. 1986. Friends and future selves. *Philosophical Review,* 95(4), 547–580.

————. 1991. Impersonal friends. *The Monist,* 74(1), 3–29.

Wiggins, D. 1980. Deliberation and practical reason. In A. O. Rorty, ed., *Essays on Aristotle's Ethics,* pp. 221–265. Berkeley: University of California Press.

————. 1991. A sensible subjectivism? In *Needs, Values, Truth,* 2d ed., pp. 185–214. Oxford: Basil Blackwell.

Williams, B. 1973a. Deciding to believe. In *Problems of the Self,* pp. 136–151. Cambridge: Cambridge University Press.

———. 1973b. Morality and the emotions. In *Problems of the Self*, pp. 207–229. Cambridge: Cambridge University Press.

———. 1981a. Internal and external reasons. In *Moral Luck*, pp. 101–113. Cambridge: Cambridge University Press.

———. 1981b. Persons, character and morality. In *Moral Luck*, pp. 1–19. Cambridge: Cambridge University Press.

Winograd, T. 1972. *Understanding Natural Language*. Edinburgh: Edinburgh University Press.

Winters, B. 1979. Believing at will. *Journal of Philosophy, 76,* 243–256.

Wolldridge, D. 1963. *The Machinery of the Brain*. New York: McGraw Hill.

Index